1963

DE SANCTIS ON DANTE

De Sanctis on Dante

Essays Edited and Translated
by
JOSEPH ROSSI
and
ALFRED GALPIN

The University of Wisconsin Press

Madison, 1957

Published by The University of Wisconsin Press,
430 Sterling Court, Madison 6, Wisconsin

Copyright © 1957,
by the Regents of the University of Wisconsin.
Copyright, Canada, 1957.
Distributed in Canada by Burns and MacEachern, Toronto

Printed in the United States of America
by Vail-Ballou Press, Inc., Binghamton, N.Y.

Library of Congress Catalog Card No. 57-9816

Preface

THE text of the *Saggi critici,* from which all the following essays are taken, was established by the author during his lifetime and has since been reproduced without alteration in successive editions; the translators used the Morano edition published at Naples and edited by Nino Cortese. Except for the relatively unimportant final essay, all embody material originally presented in lecture form. Different editions may vary in the text of the citations from Dante, which with De Sanctis were usually mere notations in the manuscript. When he wrote out the quotations he apparently did so from memory, with occasional minor discrepancies which the editors have disregarded, choosing a text of Dante in conformity with the English translation, that of Charles Eliot Norton.

Even from before the Società Dantesca published its so-called definitive text on the six-hundredth anniversary of the Poet's death, in 1921, there has been on the whole a surprising degree of uniformity in the editions of the *Divine Comedy,* and most variants have concerned punctuation or spelling. Norton's translation has the advantages of being readily available, reliable, and nearly literal. Only in two passages is there a discrepancy, though a slight one, between the Norton version and the Italian cited by De Sanctis. This is in the essay on Ugolino where the critic, in citing "cruda terra" instead of the usual "dura terra," incorporates the adjective *cruel* in his own text, and later makes another lapsus as indicated in note 69.

Rossetti's translation of the *Vita Nuova* is used, but for this and other texts occasionally cited, the translator is indicated in the footnotes, which also include all relevant bibliographical data.

The translators take pleasure in expressing their gratitude to Professors Julian E. Harris and Gian Napoleone Giordano Orsini of the University of Wisconsin, and Gusta B. Nance of Southern Methodist University, who read the translation in its initial stage and offered valuable suggestions.

J. R.

A. G.

June, 1957

Translators' Introduction
Francesco De Sanctis

FRANCESCO DE SANCTIS, the founder of modern Italian literary criticism, was born on March 28, 1817, in Morra Irpina, a small town in the province of Avellino, east of Naples, which has since been renamed Morra De Sanctis; he was the second of seven children of Alessandro De Sanctis and Maria Agnese Manzi. His family was cultured, moderately well-to-do, and liberal in politics; his father, a lawyer by training, was for a number of years the sole manager of the modest undivided family estate because two of his brothers—Pietro, a doctor, and Giuseppe, a priest—were in exile for their participation in the Revolution of 1821, and the other, Carlo, also a priest, resided in Naples where he was headmaster of a private school.

At the age of nine Francesco was placed in his uncle's school. At that time the Bourbon government of Naples looked upon education with scornful indifference. The official attitude toward scholarship is reflected in the epithet *pennaruoli* (pen-pushers) which King Ferdinand II applied to intellectuals. Most of the elementary and secondary schools, of parochial origin, were operated by the clergy, which also controlled the University of Naples. This institution led an anemic existence with a small and undistinguished faculty and a comparably small and uninspired student

body; students coming to Naples from the provinces were exposed
to ridicule and abuse from the populace, and from the police and
ecclesiastical authorities who had discretionary power to expel
them from the city. Nevertheless the youth of the kingdom continued to flock to Naples as the political and cultural capital of the
realm. The educational vacuum was filled by private teachers who
offered instruction in the arts and sciences as well as in the special disciplines of the learned professions. The students would
"shop around" for the courses and teachers best suited to their
needs and taste, and go to the University only for their qualifying
examinations which were generally neither extensive nor searching.

De Sanctis received all his formal education in these private
schools. He first studied for five years in the preparatory school
directed by his uncle, then for two years studied philosophy,
physics, and mathematics under Abbé Fazzini, and finally read
law for two more years with yet another Abbé, a certain Garzia.

At eighteen he had finished his legal studies and was about to
begin his practical training in law, when his uncle suffered a
stroke and he suddenly found himself in charge of the school. By
the time the school was closed two years later, De Sanctis had lost
his taste for the legal profession, and after only a few hours in
a lawyer's office he decided to return to teaching as his real vocation.

In this decision he was influenced by Marquis Basilio Puoti.
Four years earlier, at the start of his law studies, a friend had in-
vited him one evening to visit the Puoti school. Curiously enough,
De Sanctis had never heard of the well-known free school of
Italian studies which this nobleman had opened in his palace, and
the idea of studying grammar and composition like a schoolboy,
after one had completed his general education, struck him as
absurd. He accepted the invitation with skeptical curiosity, but
soon found himself captivated by the refined atmosphere of the
place, and by the charm and simplicity of the Marquis who, de-

spite his literary pedantry, had a warm, friendly, and unpreten-
tious personality.

De Sanctis soon discovered that the Puoti school was quite different from what he had imagined. Rather than a simple course
in rhetoric and composition, it was something like the Writers'
Institutes of our colleges. The students, mostly older than De
Sanctis, and some already practicing a profession, met three times
a week under Puoti's direction to discuss their compositions—
original or translations from Latin—and to read and analyze
selected masterpieces of Italian literature. De Sanctis realized that
such training was just what he needed, because his own style was
pompous and conventional and his knowledge of Italian literature
very limited. He took up the new studies enthusiastically and,
under Puoti's direction, proceeded to lay the foundation of his
intimate knowledge of the Italian classics in which, as Croce said,
he had no equal except Carducci. In a short time he became the
favorite pupil of the Marquis, who later used his influence to have
him appointed to the Military School of Naples, and still later
helped him to organize his own evening course of literature.

This course—his so-called First Neapolitan School—was perhaps the most important single factor in his development as a
critic and teacher. It was here, between 1839 and 1848, that he
actually formed his culture and developed his taste. He employed
his mornings teaching grammar to the unwilling and unruly
youths of the Military School. The rest of his time and energy
was devoted exclusively to preparing the three weekly lessons of
his private school, where he met with mature students who gave
him as much intellectual stimulation and inspiration as they received from him. With his utter candor, intellectual integrity, and
enthusiasm, he won the affection of his students and a widespread
renown throughout the city where, among hundreds of private
teachers, he was soon known antonomastically as "the Professor."
His horizon widened; his literary and philosophical background
broadened; every year he taught a new course, or rather he in-

vestigated, together with his students, a new field in the realm of letters. "It seemed," related Villari, "as if the whole school, together with the teacher, was proceeding boldly in quest of truth."

The Revolution of 1848 brought to an abrupt close this happy interlude in De Sanctis' career and proved a turning point in his life. Completely absorbed in his studies and his teaching, he had had neither time nor interest to spare for politics, until the revolution snatched him rudely from his ivory tower and brought him face to face with the political realities of his country. The contrast between the ideals of honor, human dignity, patriotism, and integrity that he had for years been holding up to his students, and their flagrant negation by the Bourbon government, now for the first time struck him clearly, and he took up his battle station with simplicity and dignity. When the barricades were thrown up in the streets of Naples, he took part in the fighting together with his students. As a result, when the reaction set in he was dismissed from the Military School and kept under police surveillance. After about a year of this he was jailed on suspicion for almost three years, then banished from the kingdom.

After a brief stay on the British-owned island of Malta, he went to Turin, the capital of the only Italian state which retained its liberal constitution after the Revolution of 1848, and which in consequence became the haven of political refugees from all over Italy. Arriving there late in 1853, he declined the subsidy granted to political refugees by the Piedmontese government, and set out to find a way to earn his own livelihood. This was no easy task. The educational atmosphere in Turin was different from that of Naples, and far less favorable to the establishment of private courses in literature; furthermore, he was unknown, for up to that time his teaching had so completely absorbed his time and energy that the sum total of his publications amounted to no more than one or two insignificant articles and a partial translation from the German of a *History of Poetry* by a disciple of Hegel, Rosenkranz.

Eventually he obtained a modest position in a girls' school and a few private pupils, and set about organizing a course of public lectures on the *Divine Comedy* of which the first series was delivered in 1854 and a second in 1855. These lectures mark the beginning of De Sanctis' serious interest in Dante and the first stage of an ambition, never actually realized, to achieve a new and comprehensive interpretation of the *Divine Comedy*. The critical principles by which such an interpretation should be realized are first suggested in his Lamennais review which appears as the seventh essay in the present volume and was written at Turin in 1855. The fifth essay is a reproduction, only slightly revised, of one of the Turin lectures, which also furnished him the basic material for those numbered III, IV, and VI in this volume.

While at Turin De Sanctis began also to contribute numerous articles to Piedmontese and Florentine periodicals, which brought him to the favorable attention of the leading men of letters in Italy, including Manzoni. His reputation as lecturer and critic rose rapidly. In 1856 he was appointed to a lectureship at the newly founded Federal Polytechnic School of Zurich, and the following year, when the Chair of Italian Literature at the University of Turin became vacant, he was considered for the post, but was rejected because of his Hegelianism.

He remained in Zurich for a little over four years, establishing friendly relations with such distinguished figures as the historian Burckhardt; the Romance scholar and Hegelian, Vischer, one of his closest friends who like Burckhardt was his colleague at the Polytechnic School; the poet Georg Harvegh; and Richard Wagner and his muse Mathilde Wesendonck. Unfortunately, the vital relationship with his pupils to which he had been so long accustomed failed him at Zurich, where many of his listeners were entirely ignorant not only of Dante but of Italian literature in general. However, he resumed there his course on the *Divine Comedy,* first presenting in simpler form the material of the Turin lectures: these, after a general introduction, had progressed through a detailed exposition as far as the opening cantos of the *Purgatory.* The Zurich course then continued this exposition through the *Paradise*. His Zurich lectures survive in the form of lecture notes taken by a friend and pupil, first published by Sergio Romagnoli in 1955 in the volume *Lezioni e saggi su Dante,* as Volume V of a projected *opera omnia* (Einaudi). This volume, with ample indices and scholarly introduction, presents everything extant that De Sanctis wrote or said on Dante, except the chapters in his *History of Italian Literature,* and is therefore the principal source to be consulted for more complete information by anyone who can read Italian.

While at Zurich De Sanctis projected a "libro su Dante" [book on Dante] of which the first two essays in the present volume are all that he ever completed. His study of Dante was interrupted, first by an important series of lectures on Petrarch, then by his return to Naples in August of 1860.

He had already been offered in 1860, first the Chair of Italian Literature at the University of Pisa, then one in Comparative Literature at the University of Turin, but he declined both in the expectation that the changing political situation would soon permit him to return to Naples. This hope was in fact realized. Upon his return, De Sanctis filled in rapid succession a number of important positions. He was first Governor of his native province of Avellino, then Director of the Ministry of Public Instruction in Naples where, in only two weeks, he completely reorganized the University, dismissing or retiring thirty-four professors and replacing them with outstanding scholars like Villari and Spaventa. The following year he was elected to the Chamber of Deputies, and soon after he became Minister of Public Instruction. In that post he fought for the secularization of public schools, resisting the pressures brought to bear upon him not only by the Clericals, who demanded the preservation of the Church's ancient privileges in the realm of education, but also by the Liberals, who wanted to exclude the Church entirely from teaching. In 1863 he also became editor of the Neapolitan newspaper *Italia,* from whose columns he advocated bold agrarian and educational reforms.

This first political interlude lasted for eight years, to the regret of many who deplored the loss thus sustained by literature. But in 1868 De Sanctis returned to his career as a critic which in the next few years attained its culmination. Working first on his notes from Turin and Zurich, he published the essays on Francesca da Rimini, Farinata, and Ugolino, together with seven other critical studies of capital importance, and recast a course of Zurich lectures as the monograph *Petrarch*. Then, finding himself more and more drawn toward his masterpiece, the *History of Italian Literature,* he abandoned plans for a separate work on Dante, saying his final word on that subject in the *History,* published in 1870–71, now readily available in English.

In 1872 he accepted the Chair of Comparative Literature at the University of Naples where he delivered four courses of lectures on Modern Italian Literature, published posthumously by his disciples under the titles *Leopardi* (1885), *History of Italian Literature in the XIX Century* (1897), and *Manzoni* (1922). Of these disciples, one in particular distinguished himself, first of all by his skill and assiduity as an archivist, discovering lecture notes and other De Sanctis papers in the municipal archives of Naples and elsewhere; he then went on to construct, on bases whose origin in De Sanctis he was the first to acknowledge, an elaborate system of critical philosophy, supported by essays in practical criticism, of a range and depth unique in any modern literature: this was Benedetto Croce (1866–1952).

Returning to politics in 1877, De Sanctis helped to organize a liberal opposition party, was twice Vice-president of the Chamber of Deputies, and twice again Minister of Public Instruction. He died on December 29, 1883, a few months after his re-election to Parliament.

In the evolution of De Sanctis' critical ideas three influences were predominant: Puoti's "Purism," French criticism, and Hegelian esthetics, which correspond roughly to the rhetorical, the historical, and the philosophic approach to literature. Of the French critics who influenced him, it should be noted that none exercised upon him an influence as prominent as that of Hegel, and that all are earlier, and of less individual significance, than Sainte-Beuve or Taine. As regards Hegel, greatly as he admired the German's depth of thought, his own individualistic temperament kept him perforce from falling into the systematic spirit which marks the true Hegelian. It would perhaps not be unjust to say that of the three influences the one that remained with him most constantly, and which corresponded most naturally to his personal temperament, was the one which a foreign reader would certainly consider the least important, that of Puoti and his school, since of the three it was the one which was essentially esthetic, and which took as its point of departure the examination of a given text rather than the exposition of ideas or facts accessory or extraneous to that text.

Adhering in the main to Renaissance theories of imitation, moralism, and formal beauty, Puoti took as models of language and style the Italian classics of the fourteenth and sixteenth centuries. He admitted reluctantly and with only partial approval a few writers of later periods, rather for their conformity to Purist standards than for any innovation they might bring. His declared goal was to purify the Italian language from the gallicisms that had contaminated it in the eighteenth century. Yet, in the pursuit of this narrow and futile goal, Puoti fostered a careful and minute study of literary texts which, in the case of De Sanctis at least, established the basis for an exceptionally intimate knowledge of the masterpieces of Italian literature. It was essentially on this basis that De Sanctis went on to create what Benedetto Croce, and others with him, found to be his most important and original contribution to the art of criticism, his masterful "esthetic analyses" or textual interpretations, of which the essays numbered III to VI in this volume are among the finest examples.

This type of analysis is radically different from the French *explication de textes*. In each essay De Sanctis gives a practical demonstration of how to apply one or more of his critical theories, which in most cases will first be elucidated. A particularly clear example of this procedure is the essay on Pier delle Vigne, where he first demonstrates two erroneous methods before proceeding to his own. Maintaining always this intimate relation between precept and practice, De Sanctis refrained from developing any organized system, and his ideas, often expressed in the relatively casual style of the lecture platform, can be shown to be inconsistent or vague if taken out of context and placed one beside the other; but they are always relevant to what he is saying at the time, in a way which is perhaps unique among the great critics of modern times.

Before he could achieve such a synthesis of theory and practice he had, of course, to seek wider fields of intellectual inquiry than those offered by Naples and Puoti. He first sought guidance in a variety of exponents of recent critical thought such as Schlegel, Villemain, Vico, and Gioberti; later, in Hegel and Hegelianism. While still at Naples and beginning thus to enlarge his horizon, he incurred Puoti's displeasure by disregarding the limits set by the Purists in selecting texts for study: he included Leopardi, Manzoni, and the Bible in his course on lyric poetry; he discussed the French, English, and Italian novels of the eighteenth and nineteenth centuries in his course on narrative literature; in his course on dramatic literature he included a study of the classic French drama and no less than twelve lectures on the plays of Shakespeare. In another course he analyzed in detail the new trends of literary criticism in France, Germany, and Italy, with special stress on Hegelian esthetics; during his imprisonment he learned German, and translated Hegel's *Logic* and the first two volumes of the *Handbook of a General History of Poetry* by the Hegelian Karl Rosenkranz.

Undoubtedly De Sanctis owed much to his eager study at that time of French and German criticism: from the French he learned the art of vividly reconstructing historical periods; from the Germans he learned to analyze trends of thought. In neither school, however, did he find the principle that clearly defined the essence of poetic activity. It seemed to him, as he said in his essay on Pier delle Vigne, that just as the criticism of the Purist could, and sometimes did, degenerate into a "vocabulary of words and idioms," so that of the French tended to become a collection of facts and that of the Germans, one of ideas. The score or so of articles which he wrote while in Turin represented an effort on his part to clarify his own personal ideal of literature, to determine the validity and limits of critical judgment, and to define his own critical standards independently of the schools—Purist, French, and German—upon which he had hitherto been dependent for critical theory. This fact explains the polemical tone prevalent in most of these articles. In criticizing the views of Janin, Veuillot, Saint-Marc Girardin, Gervinus, Lamennais, Villemain, or Lamartine, De Sanctis was actually re-examining opinions he had to some degree shared in the past, correcting or rejecting them in order to clear the ground for the formulation of principles more truly his own.

In examining these principles one must keep clearly in mind that De Sanctis, unlike his disciple Croce, never claimed to be an esthetician, nor even a theorist of literary criticism. He was essentially a working critic who theorized only to explain and justify his critical judgments. He was, in fact, a vigorous thinker who devoted much time and thought to literary problems, but he never cared to organize his ideas into a system because of his deep and abiding distrust of theories, all of which he felt were bound to degenerate into pedantry. As was said above, his theories must never be considered *per se,* but always as a function of the specific critical work of which they form a part. His terminology, never systematically organized, is therefore vague at times, and he falls not infrequently into apparent verbal contradictions, mainly because he takes his point of view according to the problem presented by the work or passage under discussion, and seldom according to any principles established *a priori.* These flaws detract but little from the essential force of his criticism or the thought underlying that criticism.

By temperament De Sanctis remained throughout his life attached to the attitudes of what might be called Romantic liberalism, believing that all of life should enter into art, that human life has its roots in the common people, and that art or poetry which no longer reflects the basic aspirations of the people, of the nation, has lost the principle by which it can be great. Believing that poetry is coterminous with life, more precisely with human life, he placed the divine and the bestial outside the realm of poetry as being outside our real experience. This same Romantic temper led him to prefer the vigorous, the intense, and the passionate. He felt that poetry, to be great, must always contain the element of drama, of struggle, stirring the human spirit to its greatest activity and vitality; hence the representation of beauty in repose gives an inferior sort of poetry, failing to stimulate the spiritual activity of the reader. He believed further that poetry is truth, but in a purely psychological sense that places him, in this respect, in the camp of the subjective Germans rather than that of the historical French: a really felt emotion, mood, or state of mind, expressed in language befitting it and developed in accordance with its own nature, is true; badly expressed or inconsistently developed, it becomes false. Such a truth must be judged on purely esthetic grounds, without reference to truth of fact or validity of ideas in the world of everyday reality. Finally, he maintained that poetry is concrete; that it is not a concept, however deep, nor a moral principle, however noble, but a concrete situation rendered in imagery such that the reader can recognize in it his own feelings and experience.

In the traditional criticism De Sanctis saw the essence of poetry placed in technical skill, in the selection and arrangement of words, sounds, and images according to set standards sanctioned by tradition. In the new criticism, risen as a reaction to the former, he saw poetry placed in the value of the moral, historical, philosophical, or sociological concepts expressed. For himself, he placed the essence of Art in Form in the Aristotelian sense: an essence achieving reality in an individual existence. In art this means the vision of a concrete situation or incident, embodying a mood, thought, or belief of the poet and expressed in terms of imagery. The moral, historical, or philosophical concepts to be expressed, and the poet's mood or ideas in themselves, before achieving artistic expression, constitute the "potency" or undifferentiated raw material of the poetic "act," and in themselves afford no valid basis for artistic judgment. The artistic judgment bears instead on the manner in which this content, or raw material, has been expressed: not merely the style or language with which the poet has clothed it, but the body he has thus given to its soul. "For me," he said, "the essence of Art is Form. Not Form conceived as costume, veil, mirror or the like, the manifestation of some generality distinct from it while casually united to it; but rather Form into which the idea has already passed, and which the individual has already achieved. That is the real organic unity of art. Now Form is not an idea but a thing, consequently the poet envisions things and not ideas. The immortal element in poetry is Form, whatever may be the idea or the content that grows out of that idea" (*Pagine sparse* [Laterza, 1934], p. 25).

The proper medium of poetry, the Image, is the creation of Phantasy, a term De Sanctis distinguished from Imagination, using the two words in a sense that is almost a complete reversal of common English usage. The Image must be clear, plastic, *corpulent*—as he called it, using an expression borrowed from Vico—with all the traits of a living being, all the flaws and imperfections of nature. Since nothing in real life is morally or logically flawless, there is therefore less poetry in what is perfect than in the imperfect, because that very perfection betrays it as an abstraction of the poet's mind rather than an apprehension of reality. "To be strictly logical, if one admits that the ideal, to be alive, must be expressed in an individual, with all its weaknesses, passions and imperfections, one is forced to conclude that the basis of art as well as of life, is not what is perfect, but what is imperfect" (*Letteratura italiana nel secolo XIX* [Morano, 1931], I, 79). Thus Francesca da Rimini is more poetical than Beatrice, and *Hell* more poetical than *Paradise*.

De Sanctis never accepted the Hegelian tenet of the eventual transition and dissolution of art into philosophy. He believed with

Vico that poetry and philosophy (or science) are antithetical activities, differing both in subject and presentation. He maintained that science presents a series of abstract concepts; poetry, a series of facts, figures, and individuals; that science studies a new principle only after the preceding one has been established and verified, and on that basis analyzes, classifies, generalizes in an attempt to determine general laws; while poetry mirrors life in its complexity, its integrity, with all its contradictions, as it strikes the senses, the imagination, and the emotions of the poet. For these reasons De Sanctis objected to the mixture of the two in allegory. He argued that allegory sets up a dualism between image and concept, between form and meaning, which divides and diffuses the reader's attention. As a result one can grasp adequately neither the one nor the other, and "through wanting a double food *is* left fasting and hungry" (*Hist. of Ital. Lit.*, i, 173).

In the selection of subject and the manner of developing it the poet need obey no general laws extrinsic to that subject. There are, however, rules inherent in the subject or situation chosen, which he must obey because, as De Sanctis says in Essay I, "a subject is not a *tabula rasa,* something on which you can imprint any shape you please. It is matter, conditioned and determined, already containing virtually within itself its own poetics, that is to say its organic laws, its concept, its parts, its form, its style." Nothing reveals the genius of the poet so much as this comprehension of his subject, this intuitive understanding of the limitations and exclusions imposed upon him by the nature of his conception. In this concept of form and its poetic elaboration De Sanctis shows himself close to one of the favorite ideas of Coleridge, whose work he appears not to have known but who also owed much to German thought: "No work of true genius," says the English critic in his "Lectures on Shakespeare," "dares want its appropriate form, neither indeed is there any danger of this. As it must not, so genius cannot, be lawless: for it is even this that constitutes its genius—*the power of acting creatively under laws of its own origination."*

The critic enjoys, indeed he is bound to maintain, the same independence of any rules extraneous to the subject and to its artistic formulation. In the consideration of a work of art, the primary task of the critic is not to enjoy or to judge, but to understand. He must study the subject, the author and his times, and
bring his own mind into the closest possible communion with that
of the poet—see what he saw, feel what he felt, and relive with
him the process of artistic elaboration. Actually, the critical process
consists in retracing backward the various stages of the artistic
creation: it is the artistic process in reverse.

"The artist represents his inner world only in its vital aspects,
that is, insofar as it has expression: consequently the essence of
artistry is form. The critic, on the contrary, starts from the form
or the phrase in which that particular world or situation was
externalized, and travels backward along the same path, inves-
tigating all the psychological steps leading to that expression.
The work of the artist is exactly like that of Nature: Nature, in
fact, shows not the productive forces but only the product, which
may be termed the Form of all the potential forms it includes; and
the artist likewise produces an outer representation of inner life,
not that life itself. But, as the philosopher, starting from the visible
proceeds to the invisible, and thus explains all that which has no
form but is represented by the form, so the critic, in the presence
of the work of art, starts from the form in which the artist has expressed an image, and strives to reaffirm all the latent forces, all
the psychological processes included therein. In short, the artist
directs the inner world toward an external expression, while the
critic from an external expression divines the inner world; the one
from the inner world proceeds to the form, the other from the
form proceeds to the inner world" (*Lett. It. nel secolo XIX,* i,
277).

The esthetic judgment results therefore from the critic's determination of the poetic inner world, and its correspondence, or
lack of correspondence, to the form in which it was externalized.
The esthetic judgment should thus deal exclusively with the

Form, the concrete vision of the poet, aiming to determine solely whether this was a living experience or merely a copy of previous representations, whether it is expressed in its own language, rhythm, imagery, or patterned after some past model.

It is at this point that writing techniques, stylistic devices, and the various categories of rhetoric can be properly considered and discussed. Words, phrases, figures of speech or syntactical constructions cannot be judged as to beauty or propriety without reference to specific contexts, as the Purists were inclined to do. The only standard by which they can be judged is whether they translate faithfully, without exaggeration or mutilation, the poet's inner vision. If that inner vision stands out clearly, the poet's language and style are beautiful and proper; but if the vision appears to any degree vague, hazy, confused, then his language is to the same degree inappropriate, irrespective of whatever sanction it may find in tradition. One may note here in passing De Sanctis' often expressed preference for clarity of expression which he surely owed to his Latin formation rather than to Hegelianism.

Once the esthetic judgment is understood in these terms, it becomes evident that the objective or scientific truth, validity, or morality of the poetic vision is irrelevant. It follows that the sort of criticism which concerns itself with the truth or value of the historical or moral concepts involved in the subject, is incapable of formulating in those terms a valid esthetic judgment. However, the critic must prepare himself to enter fully into the poet's world if he is to relive the poetic experience and formulate a sound esthetic judgment. For such a preparation he must know the poet's life in time and place, his cultural formation, his ideas, beliefs, prejudices and passions, his moral standards, and his language. This documentation may be preliminary, but it is indispensable. Without it, criticism becomes merely the sermon preached by the impressionist critic on a text borrowed from the poet, or the dogmatic application of some sort of pedantically conceived "code of literature" by the traditionalist critic.

But while the work of art *per se* is subject only to the esthetic judgment, it is at the same time an historical document, subject as such to judgments of a moral, historical, or philosophical nature which the critic has the right and duty to consider. The essential thing is to keep the two sorts of judgment separate. De Sanctis admired Berchet, Rossetti, Niccolini for their patriotic sentiments, but condemned them as poets; he rejected Leopardi's pessimism, but considered his poetry well-nigh perfect. "It is true," he wrote, "that the poet is not only a poet but also a man, a citizen, a thinker, a worshiper, and is accountable for what he writes—but for reasons extrinsic to his art. The fault of commonplace critics is to confuse the two, and to approve or disapprove according to the value of the content" (*Pagine sparse,* p. 25). And elsewhere, criticizing the formula "Art for Art's sake," he observed that it is true that the concern of the artist is art; that art has its own end; that the artist, like the bird in the sky, sings for the pleasure of singing. "But," he added, "the bird, with its song, expresses all of itself—its instincts, its needs, its nature. Man also expresses all of himself in his song. It is not enough for him to be an artist; he must be a man. What can he express if his inner world is poor, artificial or mechanical? Art, like nature, is production, and if the artist supplies the means of production, the man must supply the force" (*Saggi critici* [Morano ed.], III, 225).

Thus morality, excluded from the *esthetic* judgment, returns with full authority in the total estimate of a poem, writer, period, even of an entire national literature. De Sanctis the critic, after passing on the esthetic value of the work, yields to De Sanctis the man and the statesman in the broader task of placing it in total perspective. So in the *History of Italian Literature,* the greatest single work in Italian literary criticism, the moral judgment is always present, implicit or expressed, but never intrudes on the esthetic judgment passed on an author or on the tendencies of a period.

The principles and attitudes just analyzed are drawn from a consideration of De Sanctis' entire critical production. It is only natural, however, that an Italian critic's gifts, and the validity of his critical principles, should find their touchstone in application to the greatest work of Italian literature. De Sanctis' essays on Dante show with remarkable clarity how he elaborates his principles and applies them to the specific work of art.

Continuing for a moment to consider these principles in their process of chronological evolution, we may say that the first two essays in the present volume, and above all the one on the subject of the *Divine Comedy,* first crystallize the critic's ideas in the essentially new and original form that they were to retain thereafter. Considering Dante criticism before and again after De Sanctis, it can be said that his radical innovations are found first in this new definition of the subject of the *Divine Comedy,* then—as always with our critic—in the application of his method to concrete cases as in the famous essays on Francesca, Farinata, and Ugolino. Compared to these latter, models of esthetic analysis, the method followed in the *History* represents a step backward toward French and German influences. This was scarcely to be avoided, since these influences had guided him in his original quest for a proper perspective by which to situate literature in the world of historical fact and in the parallel world of ideas.

The reader who wishes to study in further detail the application of De Sanctis' method to the study of Dante, should begin with the following essays and then read the relevant chapters in the *History;* a synthetic summary of all this material would, in the limits of the present introduction, risk engendering confusion rather than clarity. Indeed, the translators have chosen to arrange these essays strictly in the order that they would have as a commentary, beginning with an introduction in essays I and II, proceeding through *Hell* from Francesca in Canto V to Ugolino in Canto XXXIII, and finally presenting as a sort of appendix the essay on Lamennais, of more general nature, which incidentally carries us some way forward into *Purgatory* and *Paradise.*

Some further comment before closing may be of value in putting these essays into perspective.

In his Dantean criticism De Sanctis took his cue from Vico. He

agreed with his great compatriot in maintaining that the best commentary on Dante is a brief and clear explanation of the things,
events, and persons mentioned in the poem, explaining then the
poet's feelings, "entering," as Vico put it, "into the spirit of what
he wanted to say," in order to understand the beauty of his poetical
language, "disregarding all ethical considerations, and, even more,
all scientific questions." For this reason De Sanctis repeatedly expressed his impatience with those commentators who explained at
great length questions of politics, philosophy, or science which had
little or no direct relevance to the poem or to the given context of
it. "Leave those disputations," De Sanctis advised in his essay on
Francesca, "to the idlers of convents and coffee houses, put aside
your commentaries, and get accustomed to reading your authors
without any intermediary. What you fail to understand is not
worth understanding; only that which is clear is beautiful. Above
all, if you wish to appreciate Dante, make the necessary studies in
literature and history and then read him without any commentary,
with no company but his own and disregarding any meaning but
the literal."

As has already been indicated, De Sanctis was by temperament
a true Romantic and had a distinct preference for the energetic
expression of passion as in Shakespeare, Goethe, and Byron. To
him, great poetry was the dramatic representation of passion,
while the representation of a serene type of beauty lacked life, was
necessarily an inferior sort of poetry. He recognized and pointed
out that it would be absurd to expect in *Purgatory* and *Paradise*
the same kind of poetic beauty found in *Hell,* but his personal
preference was always for *Hell* and for the great characters of the
Incontinent and Violent. Here passion has full sway, while in the
Frauds and Traitors of the lowermost circles passion has degener-
ated into vice, losing its original spontaneity and vitality. This
preference for *Hell,* consistent with De Sanctis' conception of
poetry as essentially concrete, was further indicative of his leaning
toward realism, with its precise and minute analyses. From this
realistic bent may be derived his often repeated assertion that

Dante's characterizations, admirable as they are, are sketches rather than full-length portraits, images roughly blocked out rather than finished statues such as those which had to await the coming of Shakespeare for full realization.

Though he never went so far as Vico in claiming that a Dante ignorant of philosophy and theology would have been an even greater poet, De Sanctis like Vico saw in the *Divine Comedy* a regrettable antinomy between Dante the thinker and Dante the poet, or, as he sometimes put it, between Heaven and Earth. In this constant struggle between the poet and the thinker, the latter at times—though not often—prevails, and his dominance results in the arid or unpoetic portions of the poem.

More recent and subtler analyses of the *Divine Comedy* have recognized this dualism of structure and poetry without seeing in it any lack of harmony. They recognize that it can and must be analyzed and understood for a full appreciation of the poem, and that the poetry of Dante is not only unimpaired by this dualism, but quite inconceivable without it. Following the lead of the Poet himself, these critics have learned to resolve the initial contradiction into a higher synthesis, by a process comparable to the Hegelian *Aufhebung* (in Italian, "superamento"). For a brilliant "superamento" of De Sanctis' concept of dualism in Dante, one should consult the extremely important work of Croce, *La poesia di Dante* (notably in the fourth edition [Bari, Laterza, 1940], p. 191).

While De Sanctis himself failed to resolve this antinomy, it remains his great merit to have seen so clearly the distinction between structure and poetry, and to have insisted on the necessity of differentiating between Dante the poet, whose value is changeless and eternal, and Dante the philosopher, the political or religious thinker, whose ideas are bound up with a particular time, place, and mode of thinking. "Muor Giove, e l'inno del poeta resta" (Jove dies, the poet's song survives), as Carducci put it in the closing line of his sonnet to Dante. De Sanctis further insisted that the literary critic's task is to separate, to "liberate" the poet from the thinker, so that the *esthetic* judgment may not be contaminated with ideas which, valid in other contexts, are irrelevant to the understanding of a specific work of poetry. But his precept alone would not suffice to make him a great critic, if he had not demonstrated how to interpret Dante's poetry with his penetrating analyses of specific episodes of the poem. Here he shows with unrivaled clarity how a certain idea, belief, or impression in the Poet's mind is transformed into a sentiment, an image, a character or trait of character—and becomes poetry.

It was especially for these analyses that Croce called De Sanctis' criticism a "milestone" in Dantean studies. Much has been written during the past century to enrich our store of knowledge concerning Dante's times, his ideas, and his culture; but of this, little has affected the validity of De Sanctis' interpretation of the *Divine Comedy,* and nothing has invalidated or essentially modified the new direction he gave to Dantean studies. Among the many called to interpret the *Divine Comedy,* De Sanctis is surely one of the chosen few whose interpretations have proved worthy of the poem.

Contents

DE SANCTIS ON DANTE

I

The Subject of the Divine Comedy

EARLY critics did not and could not understand Dante.[1] The *Divine Comedy* stood too far above their rules, too far outside them. Accustomed to judge a work by its conformity to established models, they did not know what place to assign to a poetry so original; believing that form consisted in style and language—which are simply its material means—they found its form still crude and coarse. This explains their preference for Petrarch as it does the manner in which the *Divine Comedy*, after long being unintelligently admired, fell into virtual oblivion. It was still quoted, still admired, as if by tacit agreement. *Sit Divus, ne sit vivus.* They kept on calling it divine, but quit reading it.

The first modern critics, as romanticists, were biased and opinionated; this period of exaggeration is now past. Rising from controversy to a sense of higher unity, they have replaced the traditional, passive respect for the ancients with an enlightened admiration for them; they have restored the authority of the

1. First published as "Dell'argomento della Divina Commedia" in *Rivista contemporanea* (Torino, anno iv, 1857), xi, 319–29, and thereafter in *Saggi critici* (1st ed., 1866), from which our text is taken. Based on Lectures II and III of the first year's course at Turin, and on Zurich lectures of the second semester, 1856; written at Zurich. It was destined to be the first chapter of a projected work on Dante which was never completed.

rules, which had become blind dogmatism, by relating them again to their generating principles; and they have opposed the imitation of the ancients while demanding in art at once the freshness and the truth of modern life. By withdrawing criticism from the petty disputes to which it had stooped, they have raised it to the contemplation of art in its essence and made it a science. They now proclaim the truth and independence of art and the freedom of form: in the name of truth, they proscribe all the literary and factitious elements that have crept into art; in the name of independence, they eliminate all those religious, political, and moral aims which mislead conventional criticism; in the name of freedom of form, they have learned how to appreciate and assign to its due place every true greatness, Homer's as well as Dante's, Shakespeare's as well as Racine's.

But these critics are not entirely free of the defect noted in the older school: they, too, often judge *a priori;* they set up certain general rules and measure everything by that standard. We already have a metaphysics of the beautiful which goes under the name of esthetics. From it critics have extracted and put into circulation a score or so of formulae which, detached from their generating principle and repeated on every occasion, are gradually losing all serious meaning, no longer understood by those who utter them and irritating to those who hear them. You can no longer discuss a work without having dinned into your ears such terms as dignity, order, decorum, elegance, purity; or finite and infinite, real and ideal, social literature, historical or philosophical literature, poet, painter, sculptor, musician, Idea and Truth, the Good, the Beautiful.

General rules are mere abstractions when viewed apart from a given subject matter to which alone they apply. They are applicable to the creations of art as they are to individuals in real life or to any category of the mind, but in each case they are subject to specific conditions and limitations which make each individual case what it is and not something else. Therefore, the essence of a subject is not what it shares with all other literary or artistic subjects, but what is peculiarly and incommunicably its own. A subject is not a *tabula rasa,* a thing on which you can imprint any shape you please. It is matter conditioned and determined, already virtually containing within itself its own poetics, that is to say its organic laws, its conception, its parts, its form, its style. It is a little world concealing in its bosom great treasures visible only to the poetic eye. A mediocre talent either fails to see anything at all, or sees only fragments of its riches, and by adding to it something extraneous, spoils it and does it violence. But the real poet yields lovingly to his subject, is carried away by it, buries himself in it, so to speak, and becomes its very soul, forgetting everything in his own nature that is not in harmony with it. You must fall in love with it, live in it, turn yourself into it; and then you shall see it, as if animated by your gaze, gradually moving and unfolding in accordance with its nature and revealing all its riches.

We shall try, therefore, freeing our mind of all preconceptions, to contemplate the Dantean world, to question it patiently, to call it back, insofar as we are able, to a second life. For the positive task of the critic is to relive, in his own way and with different means, the creative experience of the poet.

In Dante's time, epic narratives grouped around a few traditional characters—a king, a hero, paladins—were the fashion outside of Italy. Only later did the Italians take them in hand, and then only to make light óf them while immortalizing them with a perfection of form unknown to the other nations.

As Italy lacked a Cid, an Arthur, a Charlemagne, so it lacked traditions of chivalry and feudalism. From this some critics, like Wegele, have too hastily concluded that it lacked national traditions, but there is a vast difference between the premises and the conclusion.

The traditions of chivalry derive from the early history of those whom the Italians at that time called "barbarians." The history of Italy, during a part of the Middle Ages, was the history of these, her conquerors. Later came an age of liberty and culture: the people waged war on the castles, the cities organized themselves into commonwealths, refusing to bow even to the

Emperor. Now, this people that won its freedom was not the Goth, the Saracen, the Norman, or the Lombard; it was the conquered people, the Italian people, which had maintained a sense of national identity throughout all those invasions. It is a noteworthy fact that the Gauls became Franks; the Britons, Anglo-Saxons; the Spaniards were profoundly transformed by the Arabs; but the Italians remained Italians. And when, after a long and silent serfdom, they became their own masters; when, with the spread of a certain culture throughout the country, they were able to formulate their ideals; then they did not seek their traditions in the times when their homeland was under a conqueror's heel, but leaping over the Middle Ages which they considered an age of oppression, darkness, and barbarism, they went straight to the history of Rome as to their own.

The *Reali di Francia*,[2] for instance, widely read and distributed throughout Italy, inspired no literature. We awoke to find ourselves still Romans. So long an interval of time, such portentous events, were not strong enough to cut us off from that past which was ours. We were transformed but unaware of the change, believing ourselves to be still the same Roman people, masters of the world. With Roman pride we still called all foreigners "barbarians." No address was made to the Emperor without some mention of the grandeur and glory of Rome. Cola da Rienzo harangued like an ancient tribune. The historian never began his story without lingering a while on those pristine days. The Florentine boasted of his Roman origin. Even old wives told tales, not of Charlemagne or Arthur, but

De' Troiani e di Fiesole e di Roma.

Of the Trojans, of Fiesole, and of Rome.—*Paradise*, xv, 126.

These traditions had an important political significance in Dante's time; the Ghibelline party was founded on them, and Dante availed himself of them to support his own system in the *Monarchia*. He wished to continue the story of the Roman

2. A lengthy prose romance by Andrea da Barberino (1370–1431?), still read in Italy, which relates the mythical origin of Charlemagne and his Paladins.

Eagle, to revive and perpetuate our past. At the base of those traditions was the *Aeneid* of Virgil, which combines the story of the origins of Rome with a glorification of the Empire. To it was added Roman history, mixed with the errors, customs, and opinions of Dante's time.

But while the poets of other countries could fashion epic tales out of traditions not basically inconsistent with their own times, our Poet was separated from our traditions by differences in religion and ways of life. Traditions, after all, do not consist in mere facts; they have their inner life in religion, customs, institutions, and doctrines which now for the most part were so dead that no poet could revive them. Hence those traditions could inspire nothing of essential value to literature; they contributed only accessory elements which contrasted, often grotesquely, with the living present.

Apart and aside from these memories was the fact of contemporary life, with the Christian ideal at its center. But while, with other peoples, this ideal could fuse with their national traditions, could descend to earth and mingle with their passions, with their vital interests, in Italy it remained as it was bound to remain, outside our national past. Thus we did not develop a type of poetry like the poem of chivalry, in which tradition and religion were molded into poetic unity. We had two purely religious types, the *Vision* and the *Legend,* dealing with the supernatural or marvelous. The first presented it in terms of the afterlife; the other in terms of miracles performed on earth. The two types often merged, the Vision penetrating the Legend and increasing the element of the marvelous in it. Cavalca's *Lives,* Passavanti's stories, the *Little Flowers of St. Francis,*[3] offer many instances of this fusion, besides the long list of visions given us by Labitte,[4] Ozanam, and Kopisch.

The emotion that dominated in these visions was generally

3. A late fourteenth-century collection, author unknown, of exemplary stories from the lives of Saint Francis and his early associates.

4. The work referred to here is *Les poètes franciscains en Italie au XIII siècle, suivis de recherches nouvelles sur les sources poétiques de la Divine Comédie* (Paris, 1852).

the one best calculated to impress rude imaginations, terror. The Devil had the leading role, and the authors vied in ferocity in inventing the punishments of Hell and of Purgatory.

From the pulpit and the written page the visions soon passed into the market place; they were transformed into dramas and performed in public. The Devil, the damned and the penitent souls must have made as vivid an effect on the spectators as had the terrible Eumenides of the ancients. There was in all this a tragic concept, the damnation of the soul, presented in specific actions, in part narrated, in part acted out, as at the beginning of Greek drama. Now Dante took this subject, of which earlier writers had only glimpsed a fragment here and there; he took it, grasped it in all its breadth, and put at its base the concept of the soul's redemption. Thus the tragedy was transformed into a *comedy,* which later generations called "divine."

This subject is the final page of the human story; to use the language of poetics, it is the denouement of the earthly drama. The curtain has fallen; the gate of the future is closed; the action is over; the movement of freedom is followed by immutable necessity, by an eternal present. What essentially is all this? It is the death of liberty, the annihilation of history.

It is a perfect world, the last word of God, the final creation made in His image, in which matter is completely subdued by spirit. There is no accident, no mystery, opposition, or contradiction. Everything is determined, everything is set according to a pre-established and visible logic, according to the moral ideal. The antinomy of real and ideal vanishes, the two terms have become identical. Hence art cannot reduce to its own terms this alien world sprung from pure thought and aware of its origin. Thought persists above form and no effort of the poet can make poetry rise from this prosaic substratum. Poetry, daughter of Heaven, should descend to earth and become incarnate; here she leaves the earth, soars above the human, above history, becomes a disembodied spirit, as immobile as a mathematical symbol, becomes Science.

Our poet does not grasp this world in its immediacy, but must construct it himself from theological and philosophical concepts, according to Aristotle and Saint Thomas. He must be the philosopher and architect of his world before he can be its poet.

Here Nature is not the mysterious handiwork of God, the veiled Isis. Here you no longer have the fleeting phenomenon which, in the little it reveals, allows a glimpse into an unknown beyond, unattained and forever unattainable, the greatest charm of poetry. Here appearance and substance are one: you are in the realm of Truth. The veil is transparent; the chaste secrets of Nature, the shadings of color, of light and dark, the false and half appearances, the contrasts, the individual features—all this is destroyed. On earth, Nature stands aloof from the varying interplay of human passions. This discord art at times attempts to overcome by calling with passionate illusion on Nature to share our joys and sorrows, or at other times accepts as the expression of a higher dissonance, of the indifference of Fate to human misery.

> . . . Roma antica ruina;
>
> Tu sì placida sei?
>
> . . . ancient Rome declines; so unmoved art thou? [5]

Here the discord no longer exists. Nature becomes here the stage which the poet sets for his play, a perfect image of the idea, an emblem of thought. The enigma vanishes, taking with it a whole world of poetry.

As accident is destroyed in nature, free will is likewise destroyed in man. In this world of immutability there can be no action, for it would be an absurdity. Clashes, intrigues, vicissitudes, catastrophes, all that which is the usual subject of poetry, no longer have any meaning. Consequently, there can no longer be an action gradually unfolding in the midst of opposing forces, arousing interest and suspense, as in the *Iliad,* the *Orlando,* and in similar poems and romances which are read so eagerly, in a

5. Giacomo Leopardi, *Canti,* "Bruto Minore," ll. 82–83.

single breath, as it were. You have instead separate scenes, each complete in itself; no sooner does one character awaken your interest than he suddenly disappears before your eyes, making way for another. Not only has all action ceased: every tie that binds men on earth is dissolved. There is no place here for fatherland, family, riches, dignities, titles, customs, fashions— every element in society which, however artificial and conventional, plays so great a role in poetry. Man stands here naked— Philip the Fair without his purple [*Paradise,* xix, 120], and Nicholas III without his tiara [*Hell,* xix, 31]. What then is left to man? A general feeling of joy and sorrow, without succession, without gradation, without contrast, without echo, a sort of interjection. You have an eternal repetition. Here man fades into nature and nature into science.

Such is the subject. An epic is impossible because there is no action. Drama is destroyed at its roots because there is no liberty. The soul is as if stricken with paralysis and endures eternally in the state in which the affliction struck it. There is no clash of characters or passions; here man is dead—man as endowed with freedom, will, power, action. The lyric is reduced to a single string that repeats its solitary refrain, resembling rather the vagueness of music than the clarity of speech. What remains is existence in its changeless external traits, a mere object of description; even man is merely described, the poem remains in essence descriptive and didactic.

We have, then, two subjects: one, purely religious, thrusts poetry outside humanity, the other, historico-political, rests on traditions radically inconsistent with modern life. Hence, we have two poetic conceptions, each incomplete: one turns its back on life, the other blurs it by introducing discordant elements.

It is useless to dispute as to which of these two subjects came first to Dante's mind: namely, whether his passionately held political opinions led him to find the other world a fitting medium for their manifestation, as some believe, or whether the other world, as I am inclined to think, was first and seriously conceived for its own sake.

Be that as it may, Dante fused these two subjects, making of himself not merely the spectator but the protagonist of his world. A living man, he pierces the realm of shadows, brings to it all his passions as a man and a citizen, makes even the tranquil vaults of heaven shake to the echoes of human agitation: thus drama returns, and time is reborn amid the eternal. The Poet is like a bridge thrown between heaven and earth. At the sight and words of a living man, the souls are reborn for an instant, feel anew old passions, see again their fatherland, their friends. From the womb of the infinite springs again the finite. History reappears, and with it, characters and passions. Stirring amid the fixed woof of the future, Italy, indeed all Europe of the fourteenth century, lives and moves with its pope and emperor, its kings and its peoples, with its customs, errors, passions. It is the drama of that century staged in the next world and written by a poet who is himself one of the actors.

By means of this happy conception poetry embraces all life, heaven and earth, time and eternity, the human and the divine, the most abstract concepts and the most concrete reality. The doctrinal and mystical aspect of the next world is partially softened, and a poetry founded upon the supernatural becomes profoundly human and earthly, taking a distinctive imprint from the author and his time.

Earthly nature appears in the midst of the supernatural in the form of contrast, comparison, reminiscence; we see again our valleys, rivers, mountains, our cities and fields. The earth, transported to the other world, communicates to it something immediate and tangible, gives it a homelike atmosphere, and at the same time becomes there somehow more solemn, more ideally beautiful.

Accident and time, history and society reappear with all their inner and outer life—religious, moral, political, and intellectual; hence there takes shape in the bosom of the other world the epic, the national heroic poem. It is the poem of humanity and also the poem of Italy. Dante can represent Italian traditions without being obliged, like other poets, to do violence either to antiquity or to modern life. In the afterlife social or national differences have vanished, all men are made equal by a common destiny. There is similarity of soul, not of appearance, title, or fatherland: Alexander can well stand next to Ezzelino [*Hell,* XII, 107, 110], and Brutus can abide with Judas [*Hell,* XXXIV, 62, 66].

Contemporary history can be paraded against this background of ancient traditions. The Pope, the Emperor, the King of Naples, the Cerchi, the Donati, the wraths and ambitions, the discords and customs of the time—such is the picture to which the Virgilian tradition can now serve as a magnificent framework.

Man is no longer motionless, and becomes flesh again. He is concerned about his memory on earth; he grieves or rejoices over the tidings he hears; he threatens, grows angry or revengeful; he preaches, admonishes, satirizes, and eulogizes. Passions, characters, earthly interests are reborn in all their manifold variety.

The Poet can portray himself to us in his most intimate and personal traits, in his loves, his hatreds, his private life. While striving toward a universal goal he can seek personal aims also, without thereby altering the unity of his world. He becomes the center of his own creation, its lyrical cry, its passionate echo.

Thus an infinite variety springs to life in a subject that by its nature is narrow and monotonous; there is now a place in it for everything in life, even the most transitory of its aspects.

This bold conception, which few of Dante's interpreters have shown themselves capable of comprehending, has been called a mixture, and qualified as strange and barbaric. Unable to perceive the link that binds the two worlds, and wishing to uphold the unity of the poem, critics have regarded one world as the principal, the other as accessory. Vellutello, Landino, Schlegel,

Quinet, Ozanam, and, in part, even Hegel [6] and Schelling, consider principally the mystical and supernatural side of the subject; others, instead, view the next world as a means, an occasion, almost as a weapon which the poet has forged in order to belabor his enemies with it. This latter group would restrict the immensity and the poetic wealth of Dante's conception to a narrow, prosaically conceived political scope, carrying the exaggeration so far as to see the other world as an allegorical veil of the present. To the former group, the earthly element is an intrusion, due to the passions of the poet, so that the poem, as one of them states, results in a strange mixture of the sacred and the profane. Schlegel waxes indignant at the poet's ghibellinism; Edgar Quinet is shocked to see that the singer's earthly passions trouble even the calm of Paradise; and did not Lamartine call this poetry a "Florentine gazette"? For the others, who look principally to the historical and political aspect, like Marchetti, Troya, Foscolo, Rossetti, Aroux, the seriousness with which the Poet represents the next world, too genuine for an allegory, is very embarrassing. Thus the two schools sacrifice one world to the other. Dante intended to put into his poem both heaven and earth; they see only heaven, or only earth.

What is this poetry? It is human life viewed from the other world.

Life has inexhaustible wealth and, depending on your point of view, it reveals to you new sensations, new emotions, new aspects. If the horizon changes, the view changes with it; the same things appear to you with a different face; you seem to have acquired a sixth sense which reveals a new world and brings it before your eyes with all the freshness and wonder of first impressions.

Dante has added this new sense to poetry by changing its point of view. Ordinary poetry has its abode on this earth; the celestial beings descend to earth, mingle with men, become actors.

6. See his *Aesthetics,* Bk. ii, Ch. i. Hegel exercised a paramount influence in the formation and development of De Sanctis' critical ideas.

Dante, by transporting earth to heaven, has reversed the basis. The other world transforms bodies into shades; the emotions, the grandeur and pomp of the earth, become shadows; history is transfigured and spiritualized. The most commonplace persons, the most unimpressive things, acquire a meaning and become poetry when envisaged from the other world. Ciacco and Taide, with the seal of eternity on their brows, attain ideal proportions and arouse feelings they would not excite on earth. Contemporary history resists poetic treatment because it portrays a reality without shadows, with fixed outline, refractory to the imagination; but when placed in the other world its reality quivers before you, becomes transfigured; the best known characters acquire a different aspect as they stand before you on the pedestal of the infinite. Farinata, appearing as a contemporary of Capaneus, is viewed in a perspective of two thousand years. The marvelous comes forth by itself, without any need of being sought for, by virtue of the situation alone. You have new attitudes, new sensations, and new ways of expressing them.

What is this poetry? It is the earth seen from the other world. You may add: it is the other world seen from the earth.

In vain will you tell the Poet: "You are entering a temple; divest yourself of your passions, purify yourself, turn your back on mundane interests." He will say the same himself, and repeatedly; but he will do nothing of the sort. The earth pursues him even within the sanctuary; in the very presence of God he curls his lips to sarcasm and hurls a last imprecation upon Florence:

> . . . al divino dall'umano,
> All'eterno dal tempo era venuto,
> E di Fiorenza in popol giusto e sano.
> . . . (I, who) to the divine from the human, to the eternal
> from the temporal, had come, and from Florence to a
> people just and sane.—*Paradise,* xxxi, 37–39.

"Human" and "divine," "temporal" and "eternal"! Heed him not, they are abstractions of his mind. The human persists alongside the divine, and the temporal beside the eternal.

Like a traveler who observes faraway lands with his mind still possessed by his fatherland, through the memory of which he views all that he encounters, even so Dante sees the other world through the earth and through his own passions. Thus life is integrated, the other world emerges from its abstraction, heaven and earth mingle, and a poetry conceived in the heights of the most abstruse mysticism descends into the most intimate and vivid reality. Here is the greatness and the verity of the conception—in this omnipresence of the two worlds reacting upon one another, explaining and tempering one another. One world constantly follows, crosses, penetrates, alternates with the other; everything is replete with this unity. The Poet breaks the earth into fragments from which he reconstructs his two worlds, so that the reader, looking at the whole, can well say, "I have a new world before me"; but considering a detail here or there, is forced to think of Florence or of Rome. You stand in "a place mute of light" and stormy, and there suddenly looms before you the seashore where the Po descends,

> Per aver pace co' seguaci sui.
> To have peace, with its followers.—*Hell,* v, 99.

Francesca, enraptured in memories of the "happy time," strolls in memory through her beloved garden; then, coming to the kiss, the thought of Hell flashes through her mind and that kiss becomes motionless, is prolonged through all eternity:

> Questi, *che mai da me non fia diviso,*
> La bocca mi baciò tutto tremante.
> This one, *who never shall be divided from me,* kissed my
> mouth all trembling.—*Hell,* v, 135–36.

How heart-rending is this parenthetical remark, which seems to be made so casually! The two worlds meet at the instant of sin and are fused together.

Farinata, at the news of his party's fall from power, remains absorbed; his mind is concentrated on Florence when, to express the immensity of his grief, he is reminded of his fiery bed:

> Ciò mi tormenta più che questo letto.
>
> It torments me more than this bed.—*Hell,* x, 78.

In the very heart of the past, as he relives it, the present returns as a term of comparison—and what a comparison! Nothing can equal the grandeur of Farinata as the Poet, without any effort, simply by virtue of the situation, puts Hell under his feet. Poets, when they wish to represent beauty and strength on earth, are wont to borrow colors from heavenly things, in which they place the true abode of everything ideal. Here the metaphor is reality, the figure is the letter; one world is the paragon, the image, the light of the other.

If this subject is not left in its doctrinal generality, in its abstract spiritualism, that is because the seer is Dante. Other writers of visions either related them Homerically, remaining outside them, or like Passavanti they intervened to intrude moral observations; they were, for the most part, clerics and ascetics, detached from the world, inexperienced in life, alien to mundane passions and interests. Dante threw himself completely into the subject; and *Dante* means all the life of that epoch, in its various forms, summed up in a poetic soul. By becoming an essential element of his subject, Dante modified it profoundly to the advantage of his poetry.

In order, then, to complete the study of the subject, we must study Dante, an inseparable part of that subject; Dante not only as the Homer, but also as the Achilles of his world; not only the poet, but also the man.

Character of Dante and His Utopia

I CALL that man a poet who feels a whole world of forms and images stirring confusedly within him;[7] forms fluctuating at first without precise determination, rays of light not yet refracted, not yet graded in the brilliant colors of the iris, scattered sounds not yet combined into a harmony. Everyone, especially in his youth, is something of a poet; everyone has sometimes felt within him the knight-errant, has dreamed his Fairies, his golden palaces, has had, in Goethe's words,[8] some lady to protect, some villain to chastise. For most of us this state is transitory; reality snatches us only too soon from golden dreams and puts our nose to the grindstone. The world of imagination endures only in the soul of the poet, over which it takes possession, straining within, eager to break forth. Now, there is a solemn moment in everyone's life when he discovers his real self. We need an outside stimulus to receive this divine revelation, to be able at last to say, "*That* is what I was born for!" The life of Dante began the

7. First published as "Carattere di Dante e sua Utopia" in *Rivista contemporanea* (Torino, anno vi, 1858), xii, 3–15, then in *Saggi critici* (1866), from which our text is derived. Written like the preceding essay at Zurich at a time when De Sanctis was struggling to go beyond the Hegelian type of purely conceptual criticism. (Cf. Introduction to Einaudi edition, 1955, of his *Lezioni e saggi su Dante*, pp. xli–xlii.)

8. Goethe, *Der neue Amadis* (1774).

moment his eyes met those of Beatrice; and when he saw her a
second time, when in the heat of emotion he recalled the powerful impression she had made on his still boyish spirit, then art
was revealed to him and he knew he was a poet.

It is principally through love that the poet can realize and
allay the vague world of images that storms within him, because
other ideals that deeply stir the soul, like glory, liberty, fatherland, cannot be represented unless they are given a human
likeness. In love a soul discovers itself in another soul; in love
alone, what elsewhere is a figure becomes a reality. Read the
Vita Nuova, the first intimately personal narrative in modern
times, read Dante's lyrics! You will find *canzoni* and sonnets
inspired by some real event which, like a flint, strikes sparks
from his soul; some event insignificant and commonplace in
itself, but affecting most powerfully the lover's heart. A greeting,
a chance encounter, a glance suffice to arouse in him ecstasies,
visions, raptures, frenzies of ineffable emotion. Nor is this surprising: because his feeling is infinite and invisible, the lover can
find his own reality only in the beloved, whose least trifle—a glove,
a flower, a smile—will cause all his heartstrings to respond.

Beatrice died, and after lamenting her loss for a time, and com-
memorating it in song, Dante turned to practical affairs and
politics. Peaceful studies and young love were succeeded by
family cares and political passions; Dante the artist became
Dante the citizen. In this field a man usually discovers his own
character, acquires full consciousness of his personality and
strives to impose it upon others. One man's personality may be
weakened in the struggle against obstacles, another's strengthened.
In this power of resistance lies mainly what we term a great
character. But there are different sorts of greatness. There are
men of action, born to rule, who know how to stoop and
blandish in order to draw others to their side more easily; who,
keeping their goal constantly in view, are nevertheless able to
assume countless deceptive appearances, and though misunderstood by the multitude who call them fickle, are conscious in

their own hearts of having always been true to themselves. Dante
did not possess this kind of greatness. He was not a born party
leader, and he resembled Cato rather than Caesar. Men with
this disposition are born unlucky, always admired but never
heeded.

> Giusti son due, ma non vi sono intesi!
> There are two just men, but they are not heeded there!—
>   *Hell,* vi, 73.

Inflexible and severe, he was a man of passion and conviction.
He could neither comprehend nor tolerate the vices and errors
of his contemporaries; nor could he turn them to his own advantage, nor throw himself into the struggle of selfish interests, hypocrisy, and violence, in order to draw good out of evil, as
those who wish to rule are forced to do. As a Prior he found
himself compelled to banish his best friend, in a hopeless attempt
to pacify the contending parties; he allowed himself and his party
to be overpowered by the craft and violence of the Blacks, and he
gave them time to perfect their sinister schemes by accepting an
insidious and ineffectual embassy. As an ambassador to Boniface
he succeeded only in getting himself lulled and beguiled, and
saw himself deprived of country and goods, and Florence of
freedom, almost before he knew what was happening—a sequence
of events that later became a source of unending wrath to the
poet. As an exile he did not long retain in his party the position
befitting his mind and character, and the could neither impose
his own views nor conform them to those of others. Almost
inevitably he developed a distaste for mankind, became as harsh
to friends as to foes, and eventually stood alone, a party for himself.

Some have found grounds for praise in this attitude, imagin-
ing Lord knows what hidden and magnanimous intentions; but
Dante was alone not by choice but by a necessity of his nature.
He who wishes to live among men must accept them as they are,
and he who wishes to rule them must understand them. Dante

was too scornful of all baseness, too intolerant; the present escapes the grasp of such solitary characters, but the future is theirs.

Withdrawing from action, taking refuge in study, Dante returned to the composition of his only true action, the *Divine Comedy,* whose effects transcend the narrow circle of contemporary aims and interests and whose only bounds are those of humanity and the world. There he brought together in one volume, together with the destiny of mankind, his own sorrows, his hates, his vengeance, his hopes. And I say "hates" and "vengeance" advisedly, for Dante hated and was hated, was offended and took revenge.

I cannot compare, without a feeling of sadness, the young lyric poet with the mature author of the *Comedy.* In his lyrics you see a man to whom the world is still strange and new, on whom everything smiles; his universe is all in the eyes of a woman, his virgin soul has no place for any feeling but love, his verses have not a word of hate or of rancor. And how changed is he now! His horizon has widened, he has seen many cities, many people; courts, councils, peoples, characters, passions, customs, all reality lies spread out before him like an open book. Heretofore he has contrived sonnets and ballads; experienced in life, he can now compose a poem. But the world in which he moves causes a profound disquiet in his spirit. "What seekest thou?" a friar asks him: and the tired old man replies, "Peace!" [9]—a peace he was to find only in death.

The seeds of all the passions lie dormant in a man's heart, until some spark kindles them to flame and they burst out with a violence that surprises even himself. In Dante, civic strife roused passions of great violence, hitherto unknown to him and exacerbated by misfortune. Happy the days when the artist could yield serenely to contemplation, without the profane cry of mundane interests to disturb him! Happy the Greek artist! There are times when the poet's pen is a sharp sword. Dante's poetry is a battle engaged against his enemies, his world a stage on which

9. Letter, now generally considered apocryphal, attributed to Fra Ilario.

he plays a part, singing and fighting at the same time, at once Homer and Achilles.

But the new man did not obliterate the old, and under that wrath is hidden a great treasure of love, a great tenderness under that violence. Biographers present only one side of Dante's character. Most of them show him disdainful and vindictive, while the others, rushing to his defense, try to show how every word he wrote conforms to historical truth and justice. When I read his life as written by Cesare Balbo, a writer so amiable in his severity and so dignified in his temperance, I see gradually emerging from those pages a figure of Dante all love and sweetness like a dove.

The real Dante is neither one of these simplified portraits— or rather he is both of them together. A passionate and impulsive man, of straightforward nature, he yielded completely to the fleeting impression of the moment, as terrible in his wrath as he was compassionate in his tenderness. Those who see a logical connection among the varied outbursts of eloquence or sermonizing that have flowed from his pen, waste their time and their effort. One who would write a true life of Dante must first abandon the field of polemics where in combating one extreme we are driven into another position no less untenable; one who will draw his portrait full-face, not in profile, will present him in his entirety, just as he is, with all his sorrowful alternations of love and hatred, wrath and despair, as energetic in love as in hate, conceiving both Hell and Paradise, Francesca and Filippo Argenti, Farinata and Cavalcanti; now calling his fellow citizens "bestie fiesolane" [Fiesolan beasts—*Hell,* xv, 73], then exclaiming pitifully, "Popule mi, quid feci tibi?" [O, my people, what wrong did I do thee?] [10]

We are inclined to idealize men and to imagine them cast all in one piece. He who commits a crime is immediately called a tiger. But nature is varied in her ways, and often delights in

10. From a lost epistle of Dante mentioned by the humanist Leonardo Bruni (1369–1444), one of Dante's early biographers.

contrasts harmonized by imperceptible gradations. Achilles bes-
tially outrages the corpse of Hector, and in the presence of
Hector's old father is moved to tears. Dante is so compassionate
that he swoons at the story of Francesca and Paolo, and so
ferocious that he can conceive and describe with frightful
precision the skull of one man crushed under the teeth of another.

In civilized times we learn to control gestures and words, to
preserve at all times an air of kindliness in our countenance, so
that a so-called well-bred person is more likely to commit a vile
deed than an incivility. Dante is closer to nature, and reveals
himself bluntly.

He is essentially a poetic character. His dominant trait is a
power that breaks forth freely and impetuously. Misfortune,
rather than humbling him, fortifies him and raises him still
higher. Compelled to eat the bread of others, to beg for patronage,
to endure the banter of servants, no one has ever felt more
clearly his own superiority over his contemporaries nor raises
himself higher above them. The famous letter in which he re-
fuses to return to his home with loss of honor not only reveals a
spirit never inclined to cowardice, but in almost every line shows
the mark of this noble pride. "It is not this the way of my return
to my fatherland; . . . but if another may be found that does not
injure the good name and the honor of Dante, I shall accept it
gladly. And if one cannot enter Florence in some such manner,
then I shall never enter Florence." [11]

This is the language of a great soul but a proud one; there is
a man conscious of his own greatness, "*I,* Dante Alighieri!" From
the height of his pedestal he looks down with scorn on the plebs,
on all that is plebeian, more ready to forgive a crime than an act
of cowardice. A serious and ideal nature is best apprehended in
terms of its opposites; the opposite of Dante is the plebeian.
You almost have the impression that he felt he belonged to a
race superior not just in blood and intellect, but in spirit. Yet

11. Dante's epistle "To a Florentine Friend."

there is nothing of merely passive dignity in this attitude, for his is not a coldly stoical nature: his inner fire blazes forth violently. He has the virtue of indignation, the eloquence of wrath. All the faculties of his soul break forth with passionate impetuosity. And when from his state of wretchedness he rises to his full height above the powerful who trample him, and inflicts upon them everlasting wounds, we can understand Virgil's enthusiasm [*Hell,* VIII, 45]. To be sure, he has his moments of discouragement and surrender, but in him the most piercing emotion of grief gives way almost at once to energetic resistance. With all his misfortunes, there is not a page of his work dominated by that sentiment of moral prostration, that gloom and debility that are so common among moderns. One might even say that his grief turns to wrath in the very effort of expression, so prompt is the reaction of his energetic nature. Now, this supreme scorn for all that is base, this way of building his own pedestal, of crowning his own brow, this inner grief so proudly restrained—so that while his heart bleeds his counte-nance threatens—stamp his austere figure with a moral grandeur truly colossal, reminiscent of his Farinata.

In his youthful years everything sings of Beatrice; later, when he enters public life, Florence becomes the center toward which all his thoughts converge. Finally, when he takes up with more ardent zeal the study of theology and of philosophy, his horizon widens, he emerges from the narrow circle of Florence rising toward a unity not merely Italian but human: he becomes cos-mopolitan. He looks beyond his contemporaries, thinks of pos-terity; fame is not enough, he wants glory. To be sure, as we grow old we are inclined to generalize, and what in us was personal feeling becomes maxim and sentence. But in Dante the personal element survives in a higher form. Underneath his "humanity" there is still Florence which can still arouse longing in the exile's heart, as you can tell by his very imprecations; and underneath the Beatrice of his mind you can still sense the Beatrice of his heart. Do not believe him when he professes to have no concern except for posterity, to be a fearless friend of truth. There is too much bile in his truth, too much passion in his justice. The thought of posterity is inseparable from his longing for vengeance, his hatred for his enemies, his partisanship, his hope of repatriation, from all the vital issues of his time. His passions obsess him at times amid his most abstruse speculations, and Florence, his party, his enemies mingle with his syllogisms.

And yet, even when he is patently in the wrong, even when he gives way to wrath, to accusations and unrestrained vituperation, you cannot, I shall not say scorn him—Dante is always above scorn—but you cannot feel irritated with him. You realize that his passion is always sincere, that those impulses spring straight from the heart, that he works and speaks with the most profound conviction. If he affirms that he speaks the truth, he believes he speaks the truth; if he accuses, he has faith in the accusation; and if he exaggerates, he is unaware of it.

He is the type of the proscript that has continued to our own time. With such warmth of spirit, such power of passion, he is out of active life just when he most feels the need of it. He is banished, the world goes on without him and against him, but Dante is not resigned to the situation. Plotting with a "compagnia malvagia e scempia" [an evil and senseless company— *Paradise,* xvii, 62] soon disgusts him, and the only activity of this great man consists of a few futile epistles occasionally addressed to peoples and princes, of a few treaties and settlements negotiated in behalf of his protectors. He is left outside the flow of events, a scornful spectator. His passion, intensified by inaction, explodes with all the greater violence and bitterness in his writings. Now he bursts out thunderously like a storm long held in check; now he seeks refuge in the realm of fancy and plunges into the most abstruse mysticism. He becomes taciturn, melancholy, restless, impatient. Remote from active life, seeing the realm of the real and the possible ever escape his eager grasp, he builds a world of imagination in which he arranges people and things in accordance with his desire. Such are the dreams of exiles, which most of them carry with them to their graves; but Dante's dream was immortal. ⌐

What was this dream? That is to say, what was Dante's concept of the universe? Our dreams and our aspirations are outgrowths of our opinions and of our knowledge.

Dante was very learned; his mind embraced almost all knowledge. Learning at that time was so rare, so difficult to acquire, that it was in itself sufficient to establish one's fame as a great man. And Dante was celebrated more for the abundance and variety of his erudition, than for the greatness of his mind; while few are capable of appreciating greatness of mind, anyone can pass judgment on the material fact of learning.

He mastered the whole intellectual world of his time: theology, philosophy, history, mythology, jurisprudence, astronomy, physics, mathematics, rhetoric, poetics. And when to all this you add his travels and embassies, which gave him the opportunity to know such a variety of people and things, you can affirm without exaggeration that he surpassed his contemporaries in experience and learning. Nor was his information superficial, for there is no idea that he cannot express with clarity and mastery.

Science was still a new world imperfectly explored. Antiquity was barely rising on the horizon, and men's minds were more intent on gathering than on discerning; it was the age of admiration. Men bowed to the ground before great names, and accepted eagerly any opinion to which they could attribute a noble ancestry. A mass of ideas, drawn from various sources, had thus been gradually accumulated; no one cared how consistently, for no one looked at it too critically. Most people were satisfied with a provisional synthesis of facts which, examined separately, would often appear incompatible or contradictory. But serious thinkers were not so easily satisfied; casting a penetrating glance on this jumble-heap, they strove in some cases to harmonize philosophy and dogma, in others to point out the conflict between them.

Dante was pre-eminently a dogmatic spirit. The science of the time seemed to him the last word, and he endeavored rather to master than to examine it. He knew everything, but he left on nothing the imprint of his own thought: consequently he cannot properly be called a philosopher, a physicist, a mathematician, or the like. He accepted with perfect credulity the most absurd statements of fact and a large share of the errors and prejudices of his time. With what naïve reverence he quotes Cicero and Boethius, Livy and Orosius, placing them on the same level! [12] His mind submitted to the authority of the *Ethics* as to the Bible, to Aristotle as to St. Thomas; he believed implicitly that the great philosophers of antiquity agreed with the teaching of religion, and that they were wrong not because they saw wrongly, but because they did not see everything. I cannot see where Kannegiesser, Witte, and Wegele have discovered that Dante, having lost his faith through excessive love of philosophy and fallen into the vacuum of skepticism, wished to express in his allegorical journey his recovery, his return to faith. This is judging other times by the ideas of our own. Dante's theology does not conflict with his philosophy but completes it; Beatrice is not in contrast with Virgil but above him; Dante and Faust are centuries apart.

Dante, then, expounds things supernatural in accordance with Revelation, and for the rest puts together pagan and Christian writers. A citation is an argument. Of course I do not mean to suggest that he is always satisfied with quotations; he too wishes to demonstrate, but his philosophizing is no better than his philosophy, he has the usual shortcomings of his time. He demonstrates everything, even the commonplace; he gives equal importance to all questions; he lumps together all kinds of arguments, and beside some of real value you will find others altogether childish; he is often unable to see the heart of the question, to view it from above, to sift the incidental from

12. *Convivio,* Bk. III, Chap. 2; *De Monarchia,* Bk. II, Chaps. 3, 9, 11.

the essential; he gets lost in minutiae and subtleties, and drowns you in distinctions.

Philosophy was not a vocation for Dante, not a lifetime goal toward which he directed all the forces of his spirit. It was a postulate, a point of departure. He accepted philosophy as it was taught in the schools, and acquired a complete and exact knowledge of it. Upon this groundwork he labored to erect a political system. He was therefore not a man of pure speculation; finding himself involved at an early age in public affairs, he turned his thoughts to politics.

It is remarkable that the famous contention between pope and emperor did not give rise to two different schools of philosophy. There was not a Guelf philosophy and a Ghibelline philosophy. Both parties accepted the same basic principles. There were indeed some individual exceptions, Ghibellines who pushed on daringly beyond Catholicism, but even for them the dissent lay in a certain number of more or less unimportant details, the system as a whole never being questioned by anyone. No new theology and philosophy were created.

The struggle was therefore not between two philosophies. The two parties accepted the same foundation, but each raised on it a different structure.

They accepted the distinction between mind and matter, and the pre-eminence of mind—the foundation of Christian philosophy. And, as a corollary, they accepted the principle of the two powers in society, the spiritual and the temporal, the Pope and the Emperor.

Thus far Guelfs and Ghibellines, Boniface VIII and Dante, were in agreement, but the systems they built upon that common base were different.

If it is true that the spirit is superior to the flesh, Boniface argued that it must be equally true that the Pope is above the Emperor. "The spiritual power, says Boniface, has therefore the right to institute the temporal power, and to call it to judgment

when it is not good. . . . And he who resists, resists the very
order of God, unless he fancies, as do the Manicheans, two
principles; which we condemn as error and heresy. . . . Therefore every man must submit to the Roman Pontiff, and we declare . . . . that this submission is necessary to the salvation of
the soul." [13]

Dante accepted all the premises, and in order to deny the consequence he maintained that spirit and matter were endowed
each with its own life, without interference with the other; and
from this he inferred the independence of the two powers, the
spiritual and the temporal. Having started on this path, Dante
went all the way, and built to suit himself. The people are corrupt
and wish to usurp power, society is wicked and contentious: the
only remedy is the Emperor. Dante attributes to him all the
privileges of the Pope and makes him, like the Pope, directly
responsible to God. Both are organs of God on earth, "two suns"
[*Purgatory,* xvi, 106] who guide humanity, one in the ways of
God, the other in the ways of the world, one to heavenly and the
other to earthly happiness; both are equal, except for the reverence the Emperor owes the Pope—the only concession Dante
makes to the superiority of the spirit. Rome by divine right
should be the capital of the Empire and therefore of the world.
The franchise of the communes and the independence of the
nations were to remain inviolate. The Emperor would be all-
powerful, but in his very omnipotence he would find his check.
Through him justice and peace would triumph on earth. Such
was Dante's utopia.

It was no simple return to the past, as Wegele claims. In it we
find elements of the past and of the future, progress and regression. What belongs to the past need not be indicated here.
But in it we see the germ of the liberation of the laity, and the
pathway to larger social units. You glimpse the nation succeeding

13. Lamennais, *The Divine Comedy,* "Introduction on Dante," ch. v. (Author's
note)

the commune, and humanity succeeding the nation. It is a dream which has in part become history.

It was basically the dream of the Ghibellines. Dante's merit lies in having expanded it into a system, in being its philosopher, in rising to the concept of humanity. The foundation is weak, but the edifice is beautiful by the vastness of its design and the harmony of its parts.

In any age two opposite extremes can be found, represented by parties or individuals. Seek Dante at these extreme points and you will not find him. Nevertheless, partisans insist on dragging Dante over to their side, each advancing plausible arguments. Some see in him a good Catholic, some a heretic, some a visionary, some a conservative. As they view his character from a biased position, so they see his opinions. Theirs is a Dante divested of part of himself and placed at an extreme position.

Dante reflected the feelings of the masses. As in the masses past and future stir confusedly together, so in Dante two men are mingled together, the man of the past and the man of the future. Catholic in intent, he was neither a Catholic in every respect nor was he in every respect a heretic. Inseparable from his Catholicism is the bitter war he wages against the corruption of the papacy, as are certain bold opinions already revealing a kind of vague disquiet, confused aspirations which were to penetrate the human consciousness in later ages. But basically the problem for him, as for the masses, was not religious but political. If he boiled with indignation, if he threatened, scolded, and cursed, it was because he faced, not a hostile religion, but a hostile politics. Yet even in politics he kept his ideas within a golden mean, letting Ghibelline ideals predominate but without rejecting the main tenets of the Guelfs. If indeed he wished the papacy reformed, he respected its independence; if he wanted the communes to submit to the emperor, he also insisted that their liberties be respected; if he wanted nations unified, he wanted their autonomy upheld. To be sure, the realization of his system would have destroyed all those things, but nevertheless Dante did want to keep them. The Guelfs, of course, did well to follow logic rather than Dante.

His system did not remain a pure and serene speculation like Plato's *Republic,* but took total possession of his whole being. It was not merely his conviction, it was his faith; and faith is more than mere belief, it is will, love, and labor; it is more than mere thought, it is also sentiment and action: Dante was a man of faith.

He had faith in God, in virtue, in fatherland, love, glory, in the destiny of mankind. His faith was so vital that misfortunes and disappointments could not enfeeble it; to the last he held hopes of imminent redemption, and he died with all his youthful illusions and passions intact. Who can say at what moment Dante felt old: was it when his pen dropped from his weary fingers?

Faith is love; and it is not only wisdom, but love of wisdom. It is not only Sophia but also *filosofia* [philosophy]. And philosophy was Dante's beloved, his second Beatrice, the "amor che nella mente *gli* ragiona" [the love that discourses in his mind].[14]

Philosophy is "amoroso uso di sapienza, figliuola di Dio, regina del mondo" [loving use of wisdom, daughter of God, queen of the world]; [15] when God set the spheres in motion, she was present:

Costei pensò chi mosse l'universo.

Of her was he thinking who set the universe in motion.[16]

Philosophy, then, was for Dante the science of things human and divine, the science of the world, the universal content in which he found defined all the objects of his faith—God, virtue, humanity, love, and so on. It was not only speculation on the sweetest truths, but also the foundation of his life, and he con-

14. *Convivio,* "Canzone seconda," l. 1.
15. *Ibid.,* Bk. III, Chap. 12.
16. *Ibid.,* "Canzone seconda," l. 72.

formed his conduct to its teachings. "Absit a viro Philosophiae domestico temeraria terreni cordis humilitas . . . . absit a viro praedicante justitiam . . . nonne dulcissimas veritates potero speculari ubique sub coelo?" [Far be it from a friend of philosophy this abasement befitting a heart of clay . . . . far be it from a preacher of justice . . . . can I not speculate on the sweetest truths anywhere beneath the sky?] [17] This "friend of philosophy," as he with rightful pride termed himself, did not believe in her only in the abstract, but devoted his whole life to her, was impassioned by her, enraptured in that mystical exaltation called enthusiasm.

One who sees with what fervor Dante plunges into the most profound speculations, might say, "There is something mystical about this man, something ascetic"; and this is true. But this ascetic does not stay locked in his cell, a solitary contemplator. He belongs to the church militant, he is a soldier in the service of truth. He envisages a philosophic world, and endeavors to make the world of reality conform to that image. He strives for that goal with his pen when he cannot do so with his deeds; he writes letters, treatises, poems, always with that image before him. But he finds the world too far removed from his vision, and the contrast between idea and reality perturbs and embitters him; in every page he writes, you sense not the tranquil philosopher but the warrior, made more savage by the resistance encountered.

Is his passion always the result of unalloyed enthusiasm? I shall not try to make a saint out of our hero: the heavenly spark in him is mixed with clay.

Enthusiasm is the poetry of passion; take away enthusiasm and passion becomes an animal instinct. In our passions there enter elements, often unknown to us, of pride, personal interests, enmities, antipathies, prejudices; these are purified and ennobled by enthusiasm.

You may tell me, "You are angry with such a person because

17. Dante's epistle "To a Florentine Friend."

he insulted you"; I need not blush with shame if I can reply,
"True, *homo sum,* I am only human; but I am also indignant
because he is wicked, because he is an enemy of my fatherland!"
That is a reply which Dante could always give. At times he
speaks out because he yearns to return to his fatherland, because
he longs for revenge, because he hates those who injured him.
But even in the mire you always find the divine spark, you
always find a saintly soul who stands before an ideal world in
which he believes and with which he is in love. His outbursts
are partly born of that faith, and his hatred born of that love.

Dante is one of the most poetical and most complete images
of the Middle Ages. His fiery soul mirrors human existence in
all its range, from the most intellectual elements to the most
concrete. This man, going to the next world, takes the whole
earth along with him.

Francesca da Rimini

ALMOST at the very gates of Hell we meet this Francesca, whom Dante has immortalized.[18]

For many, the whole *Divine Comedy* is just two names: Francesca da Rimini and Count Ugolino; and a handsome volume one could make indeed, if he cared to gather together all the subtleties and sophistries that have been spoken or written on these two.

Why did Dante relate so feelingly the story of Francesca da Rimini? Because, answers Foscolo, Dante dwelt in the house of Guido da Polenta, the girl's father: perhaps he saw the room she occupied before her marriage, perhaps he heard the grievous tragedy told by the family, and from that first impression must have conceived the episode, retouching and perfecting it from year to year until he brought it to perfection. And why did the poet leave the sin in shadow while setting in sharp relief all that is kind and affectionate in the sinner? Out of delicacy and gratitude, answers Foscolo: because, received as a guest in the father's

18. First published in the *Nuova Antologia* for January, 1869, under the title "Francesca da Rimini secondo i critici e secondo l'arte," and then in *Nuovi saggi critici* (1873), from which our text is derived. It represented a return, ten years after the Zurich essays, to the project of a book on Dante, abandoned under the pressure of writing the *History of Italian Literature*. The essay is an elaboration of the twentieth lesson of the first series of lectures at Turin.

house, he was loath to defame the daughter. And why—wishing to justify or extenuate her sin—did Dante fail to mention a circumstance of the greatest importance, whether factual or legendary, namely the heinous fraud perpetrated on the wretched girl who thought she was marrying Paolo, and did not realize until she awoke the following morning that the man at her side was Paolo's deformed and lame brother Lanciotto? Because an ideal representation, Foscolo answers, must not be overloaded with factual incidents which would alter its purity. And why did Dante join together the two lovers in Hell? Because, answers Ginguené, they were not, for such a slight fault, really damned at all. On the contrary, corrects Foscolo, their sin was very grave, as shown by the closing line of her story ["That day we read no farther in it"]; but greater than their sin was the mercy of God, who out of consideration for so great a love softened their punishment by permitting them to continue it even in Hell. And why the comparison with doves? Because doves are very lustful animals, promptly replies a commentator. And why does the poet let Francesca speak and not Paolo? Because, answers Magalotti with scant gallantry, women are by nature garrulous; and, continues Foscolo, guilty of taking this inanity seriously, because women under the stress of passion must speak and give vent to their emotions. And why does Dante feel so great a grief that he loses consciousness "dinanzi alla pietà de' duo cognati"? [before the pity of the two kinsfolk—*Hell*, vi, 2]. Because, insolently answers a friar,[19] he must have remembered having committed a similar sin himself.

There you have a sampler of the "whys" and "perhapses" on which Dantean commentators exhaust their ingenuity. I am told that at the teachers' conventions held in Florence, Francesca da Rimini has been much discussed, and that some have discovered the essential beauty of the canto in the line so often distorted by commentators:

19. This was Lombardi.

Quel giorno più non vi leggemmo avante.
That day we read no farther in it.—*Hell,* v, 138.

And if this is true, it must be said that criticism has made so little progress in Italy that one can still indulge in such dissertations, suited only to idle minds, fond of riddles and obtuse to the pure and immediate impressions of art.

I received, a little over a month ago, a letter signed by three students from the college at Bari. They asked me why Petrarch had written the *Canzoniere* in Italian and not in Latin, and told me they had made wagers in support of different views. I was sorely tempted to reply that Petrarch had written in Italian because Laura knew no Latin; but it seemed cruel to answer flippantly a question those boys were taking so very seriously.

And yet, if my word carried any weight with the new generation, I would say, "Leave these disputations to the idlers of convents and coffee houses, put aside your commentators and accustom yourself to read your authors without any intermediary. What you fail to understand is not worth understanding; only that which is clear is beautiful. Above all, if you wish to appreciate Dante, make the necessary studies in literature and history and then read him without any commentary, with no company but his own and disregarding any meaning but the literal. Trust to your impressions, especially the first, which are the best. Later you can elucidate them, educate your taste; but your path must not be encumbered at the outset by preconceived judgments and artificial methods."

The canto of Francesca is one of the most beautiful precisely because it is one of the clearest; and I am amazed to see commentators, before such a limpid creation, abandon themselves to riddles and guesswork and devise the most fantastic "whys" and "wherefores." I shall waste no time in refuting the absurd answers, because the error here lies not in the answers, but in the very nature of the questions. This occurs when the critic's esthetic impressions have faded away, his mind has cooled, and he, no longer capable of grasping the situation in its entirety, loses himself in details. These details, separated from the core, taken out of the whole from which they derive their motivation and their meaning, assume purely arbitrary aspects and become the ground for any gratuitous supposition that may pop into one's head. Let's clear the ground of these "perhapses" and "whys," and approach this eldest daughter of Dante with no sentiment other than artistic, and no purpose but contemplation and enjoyment.

It little matters how Dante was led to the conception of this Francesca; and it matters still less to know whether, or to what extent, he may have altered or modified historical tradition. What matters is this: Francesca, as Dante conceived her, is more alive and real than she could ever be as presented by history. And that cannot be denied. Juliet, Ophelia, Desdemona, Clara, Thecla, Margaret, Ermengarda, Sylvia[20] have a life more solid and substantial than all the women of history. The arid style of a chronicle, the gravity of history deprive the latter of all intimacy in their life and make them stand apart from us; we see them in the market place but we do not know them in their homes; we know their actions but not their hearts; whereas the creatures of poetry inspire us with a confidence bordering on familiarity: they come before us amiably and reveal to us with total abandon such secret joys, such hidden griefs. Francesca belongs to this group of immortal women; she is in fact the eldest, the first real flesh-and-blood woman to appear on the poetical horizon of modern times.

Francesca came into being only after a long elaboration in the

20. Famous fictional heroines: Juliet, Ophelia, Desdemona, from Shakespeare's *Romeo and Juliet, Hamlet,* and *Othello,* respectively; Clara, from Livre VI, 8 ("Claire") of Victor Hugo's *Contemplations:* De Sanctis had written of her in a critical essay on *Les Contemplations,* republished in *Saggi critici* (1866); Thecla, from Schiller's dramas *Die Piccolomini* and *Wallensteins Tod;* Margaret, from Goethe's *Faust;* Ermengarda, from Manzoni's drama *Adelchi;* Sylvia, from Leopardi's lyric "A Silvia."

lyrics of the Troubadours and in the early works of Dante himself. It is Man who monopolizes the stage in these lyrics; he alone acts, speaks, dreams—the woman stands remote, mentioned but not portrayed, like Selvaggia or Mandetta;[21] and even at that remote distance she stands as man's reflection, his property, his creation, the creature drawn from his rib, with no personality distinctly her own—a concept given such lofty expression in Leopardi's *Aspasia*. At times she is merely a concept on which the poet disserts or reasons, as Cavalcanti often does, and sometimes Dante too. Then she becomes a type in which the poet assembles all moral, intellectual, and physical perfection—an artificial being coldly contrived and repugnant to true art. The most original and complete poetical creature of this sort is Beatrice: beauty, virtue, and wisdom, a character disembodied and sublimated and hence no longer a character but a type or a category, not a woman but the Womanly, the Eternal Feminine of Goethe; an admirable conception, but still not truly a woman, not a real person. Even Dante's great creative gifts were not adequate to the task of fusing together the great variety of elements congregated in her, and she often seems rather a personification and a symbol than a living person.

If in these symbolic, theological, scholastic constructions we fail to find Woman, we find Love even less. Love too is often a personification, a reminiscence of Cupid. Even when it is no longer represented as a creature of myth, but shown acting directly as a force of nature, it leaves us cold despite the poet's tears and sighs, because it is too idealized. It impresses us merely with esteem and admiration for the noble qualities of the beloved, and for the excellence of the poet's form, rather than giving us a sense of flame and fury (as Ariosto would say), of the blind unconquerable force to which all must yield.

At the core of these artificial structures, based on the worship of woman placed on the pinnacle of all perfection and made into

21. The ladies sung in the poems of Cino da Pistoia and Guido Cavalcanti respectively.

a symbol of all the lofty ideals that move men, there still remains
the concept of woman visualized not only as the feminine, not
only as the beautiful form embodying all man's ideals, but also
as an individual in herself, as a loving and gentle human being.
Such an individual, free of all heterogeneous elements, no longer a
concept, or type, or personification, but a real personality, fully
individualized and fully self-sufficient, is Francesca. When Beatrice says of herself,

> E chi mi vede e non se n'innamora
> D'amor non averà mai intelletto,

> And whoso beholdeth me and is not enamoured thereat
>   ne'er shall have understanding of Love,[22]

she is at once more than a woman and less than one. One cannot
but feel here an ulterior sense, vaster and loftier than the literal
meaning. Beatrice is here more than a woman, she is "angeletta
bella e nova" [maiden beautiful and rare]; she is the divine
not yet humanized, the ideal not yet realized, the face or aspect
of all that is beautiful, good, and true, drawing to herself all
those who have power to understand her, who have "intelletto
d'amore" [understanding of love]. But that is precisely why
Beatrice is less than a woman, why she is pure femininity, the
genus or type and not the individual. That is why you may contemplate, worship, understand, explain her, but you cannot love
her, you cannot possess her in pure esthetic delight, but rather
you stand aloof from her. This explains why Beatrice has never
achieved popularity, but has remained an inexhaustible source
of dissertations and pretentious nonsense. Francesca, on the other
hand, acquired immense popularity even in the least cultured
countries, and even today she is of the whole *Divine Comedy*
the only character that has survived. Such was certainly not
Dante's intention. Confusing poetry with science, he believed that
where there was greater virtue, truth, and perfection, there also
was greater poetry; whereas it is really just the contrary, for sci-

22. Dante's ballad, "Io mi son pargoletta bella e nova," ll. 6–7.

ence inclines to the abstract, to the idea as idea, while art has
for its object the concrete, the form or idea concealed and forgotten within the image. Science is the genus and the species, art
is the individual or the person, and the farther you move from
the individual, the more you sublimate and disembody, the
farther you get from art.

Francesca is a woman and nothing but a woman, she is a complete poetic personality of Homeric clarity. True, she is ideal,
but she is not the ideal of something else; she is the ideal of herself, and an ideal perfectly realized, with a wealth of attributes
that give her all the semblance of a living person. Her traits—
love, gentility, purity, modesty, charm—are already found in all
the concepts of woman prevalent in the poetry of the time; but
in her case these traits are not mere epithets, but the true qualities of a real person, qualities that are operative and therefore
alive. Like an Oedipus unaware, Dante here kills the Sphinx and
enters into full possession of life: here before him, in Hell, is the
woman he is seeking in Paradise. Francesca is not the divine,
but the human and the earthly; she is a fragile, passionate creature, capable of sin, guilty of sin; her condition therefore is such
that all her faculties are stirred to life, resulting in deep-rooted
conflicts that stir irresistible emotions: and this is life!

Francesca has no vulgar or wicked qualities like hatred, rancor,
spite, nor has she any special good quality; she seems to have no
room in her soul for any feeling but love. "Amore, amore,
amore!" That is her happiness and therein lies her misery. Nor
does she seek to excuse her sin by invoking the fraud perpetrated
upon her, or any other mitigating circumstance: her speech has
a frightful sincerity. "He loved me, and I loved him!"—that is
all. She is convinced in her mind that things could not have hap-
pened in any other way, that love is an irresistible force. This
omnipotent fatality of passion, overpowering the soul as it draws
it, in full consciousness of guilt, toward the beloved, is the high
motive around which her whole character unfolds. It is precisely
because love is represented as a force outside the soul, of irre-

sistible power, that you have here a case of weakness and not of depravity.

Francesca remains the type from which the modern poetic imagination has derived its most beloved creations: delicate beings without the strength to resist or react, frail flowers to which the slightest breeze is deadly, all alike in these common traits. Thrown into a world they do not understand and which does not understand them, you see them, as Dante depicts them, carried "di qua, di là, di sù, di giù" [hither and thither, down and up], by the wave of their passion; and in the theater you cannot resist a sense of heartbreak as you see them draw, smiling and carefree, closer and closer to the abyss they are digging for themselves, in which all their youth and beauty will be engulfed almost before they taste the joys of life.

This is the "tragedy" of woman, varied by a thousand incidents but always in a changeless setting. Ophelia, Juliet, Clara, Thecla, Margaret, Francesca are all related, all have the same destiny stamped on their brow. Man in his struggle against fate may be vanquished, and still hold his soul untamed and rebellious, like his prototype Prometheus; or he may resist and conquer, without necessarily ceasing thereby to be a poetic character. But woman's aureole is her weakness, and if she struggles victoriously against some overwhelming passion, no moralist can make her into anything but an unesthetic character—virtuous, admirable, but unesthetic. Woman is poetical when she is defeated in her vain struggle against that iron necessity that Dante expressed with such rare energy in the phrase "Amore . . . a null' amato amar perdona" [Love . . . absolves no loved one from loving.—*Hell,* v, 103]. But in her struggle and surrender, she must preserve that indefinable essence, soft, pure, modest, and tender, which is woman, "l'essere gentile e puro" [the gentle and pure being]. A woman depraved by passion is a creature unnatural and therefore alien to us and devoid of interest. But the woman who, in the weakness and distress of her struggle, preserves inviolate the essential qualities of womanhood—purity, modesty, gentleness, exquisite delicacy of feeling: her, even if guilty, we feel to be part of ourselves, of our common nature, and she arouses the highest interest, draws tears from our eyes, and makes us fall "come corpo morto" [like a dead body].

Francesca dissembles nothing, shields nothing. She confesses her love with perfect candor, without complaining or repenting of it; she seeks no extenuating circumstances nor does she take issue with divine justice. "Paolo loved me because I was beautiful, and I loved him because I took pleasure in being loved, and was pleased with his pleasure!" These are things that ordinary women would not even whisper in your ear. She calls *beautiful body* that which kindled Paolo's love; calls *pleasure* the sentiment that "even now does not abandon" her; and when Paolo kissed her mouth *all trembling,* surely Paolo's flesh was not trembling with fear. Here you find genuine and true passion, intense and highly sensual desire; but with it you find an ennobling sentiment, a modesty that seems to bestow a kind of virginity on every act, so that in such gentility of speech you can ill discern whether you have before you the guilty Francesca or the innocent Juliet.

There is here an atmosphere of tenderness and sweetness that pervades the entire canto, an exquisite delicacy of feeling and a certain sweet softness, one could almost say feminine weakness, wherein lies the charm of such natures, and which is so well expressed in the line

Farò come colui che piange e dice,
I will do like one who weeps and tells.—*Hell,* v, 126.

so similar in meaning but so different in tone from the other line,

Parlare e lagrimar vedrai insieme.
Thou shalt see me speak and weep together.—*Hell,* xxxiii, 9.

A small gesture of sympathy that would be overlooked by
ordinary people is instead treasured by a sensitive soul. Actually,
what did Dante say?

> . . . O anime *affannate*
> Venite a noi parlar, s'altri nol niega.

> O wearied souls, come to speak with us, if Another deny it
> not.—*Hell,* v, 80–81.

One interpreter is surprised that Dante did not request them by
"quell'amor che i mena" [that love which leads them—*Hell,* v,
78], as Virgil had suggested, and a Latin translator of Dante, a
certain D'Aquino, corrects the Poet here in accordance with
the interpreter's desire. But what sort of interpreter, of translator,
is this? Theirs are deaf ears, sensitive only to the cannon's roar.
The mere word *affannate* [wearied] is enough for Francesca. It
is a "compassionate" cry, a voice alive with pity, which reaches
her in the realm where "la pietà è morta" [pity is dead—*Hell,*
xx, 28], and under that first impression she thinks instantly of
praying God, as she was wont on earth, for the man who has
"pietà del *suo* mal perverso" [pity on *her* perverse ill]. And the
prayer does issue from her lips, but conditioned by an *if* which
brings to it a simultaneous consciousness of Hell, and the realization that God is no longer her friend, that she no longer has the
right to address a prayer to Him.

> Se fosse amico il Re dell'universo,
>   Noi pregheremmo lui per la tua pace,
>   Poi che hai pietà del nostro mal perverso.

> If the King of the universe were a friend we would pray
>   Him for thy peace, since thou hast pity on our perverse
>   ill.—*Hell,* v, 91–93.

This conditional prayer that a condemned soul sends to God
from the pit of Hell is one of the finest, most delicate and
gentlest of sentiments, realistically portrayed. There is no prayer,
but the intention of prayer; there is a mingling of the earthly and

the infernal in Francesca's soul; there is a pious intention in conformity with the language and habit of a person still alive, which
yet fails to become a prayer because it is accompanied by the
consciousness of her present state.

A modern poet would have analyzed what here is but one complex and immediate moment. He might portray Francesca in a
moment of oblivion as if standing alive before a living person,
and then interrupt the prayer on her lips with a cry of "Alas
what words I spake!" etc., and a swift reversion to her actual
state, with a touch of the theatrical of reliable effectiveness. But
in so doing he would be a critic, not a poet; he would analyze
two inner and contrasting emotions which are presented here
simultaneously, one within the other, and would thereby lower
Dante's calm and synthetic presentation to the level of a rhetorical
artifice.

The same thing is done by those blessed commentators who
spoil and corrupt good taste by analytical subtleties. Francesca
says,

> Ma se a conoscer la prima radice
> Del nostro amor tu hai cotanto *affetto,*

> But if thou hast so great affection to know the first root of
> our love. . . .—*Hell,* v, 124-25.

and the commentators annotate, "*affection* here is a rhetorical
figure and means desire!" Coarse heartless people, whose interpretations deface all the most delicate beauties in the expression of
feeling. When Francesca, boldly indifferent to grammar, says
affection, she has vividly in mind not Dante's *desire* to know her
story, but rather the *affection* with which he expresses his
desire; for her sensitive spirit could not fail to notice the touching way in which Dante, calling her by name, said,

> . . . Francesca, i tuoi martiri
> A lacrimar mi fanno tristo e pio.

> Francesca, thy torments make me sad and piteous to weep-
> ing.—*Hell,* v, 116-17.

And everything in this scene is similarly fine and delicate. To die, for Francesca, is to lose "la bella persona" [the fair body], which pleased Paolo so much—a thought steeped in the melancholy of a woman in love, sweetened a little by the thought that follows, that she died together with him in "una morte" [one death]. Love was for Paolo necessity of a gentle heart, for her, necessity of a woman beloved.

> Amor ch'a cor gentil ratto s'apprende . . . .
> Amor ch'a nullo amato amar perdona . . . .
> Amor condusse noi ad una morte.
> Love, which quickly lays hold on gentle heart . . . . Love, which absolves no loved one from loving . . . . Love brought us to one death.—*Hell,* v, 100, 103, 106.

These three admirable lines sum up all the eternal story of love, as it appears to a woman. This Francesca is so gentle that when she has to express something that may displease and arouse indignation she simply states the bare fact, without any qualification, as in

> Caina attende chi in vita ci spense . . . .
> Galeotto fu il libro e chi lo scrisse.
> Cain awaits him who quenched our life . . . . Gallehaut was the book, and he who wrote it.—*Hell,* v, 107, 137.

Even in speaking of indifferent things she has something soft and sweet that reveals a noble and refined soul. Such is the effect produced by the famous lines,

> Siede la terra, dove nata fui,
> Sulla marina dove 'l Po discende
> Per aver pace co' seguaci sui.
> The city where I was born sits upon the seashore, where the Po, with his followers, descends to have peace.—*Hell,* v, 97–99.

There is in this gentle and loving soul an inborn restraint, a kind of modesty and chastity which you sense when she pauses, is silent, vaguely hints, or veils the nudity of her heart. Hence the profound impression produced by certain brief phrases that seem on the surface so unimportant, like "ancor non m'abbandona!" [it does not even now abandon me—*Hell,* v, 105], underneath which you detect the thrill of sensuality, the *pleasure,* still alive, eternally alive; or that other phrase, "e il modo ancor m'offende" [and the mode still hurts me—*Hell,* v, 102], which is obscure and therefore dubiously effective, but which suggests a crisis in her soul at the moment she was deprived of her "fair body." And then Francesca pauses, and cannot bring herself to display the nudity of passion, the sweet sighs, the sweet sin, until forced to it by Dante's affecting question; and she breaks off the story, fully concealing herself as if wrapped in a cloak, with the mysterious phrase,

> Quel giorno più non vi leggemmo avante.
>
> That day we read no farther in it.—*Hell,* v, 138.

Are they really human, the commentators who torture this poor phrase and, like friars, insist that this woman make full confession, speak what her lips cannot utter? In their attempts to give precise meaning to what must remain vague, dubious, indefinite, they are veritable impotent ravishers, striving in vain to raise the dense veil and snatch the secrets of a modest soul. It stirs my bile to see curious and gossipy vulgarians loiter about such delicate creations.

From this restraint, from this modesty and chastity of feeling, is born a style "all things," as Montaigne [23] would say, but things pregnant with emotion, with impressions, with mystery. As the fragments of ancient Rome or Pompeii make you lower your head and dream, so this lapidary style forces you, like Dante himself, to lower your head and reflect. No laments, no reproofs or regrets, no outbursts of indignation or of pathos; even when

23. Montaigne, *Essais,* III, 4.

emotion must now and then break through all restraint, it appears in a calm and impersonal form, as

> . . . nessun maggior dolore,
> Che ricordarsi del tempo felice
> Nella miseria.

> There is no greater woe than the remembering in misery
> the happy time.—*Hell,* v, 121–23.

Her impressions remain wrapped and enclosed in the things that aroused them, and their power is all the greater when, finally disclosed, they break out to echo long in the reader's soul.

Such is Francesca; and who is Paolo? Not Man, the male set up in antithesis to establish a dualism, for Francesca occupies the whole stage. Paolo is the mute expression of Francesca; he is the cord that vibrates to her spoken word, the gesture that accompanies her voice. One speaks, the other weeps; the weeping of one is the speech of the other. They are two doves borne by the same will, so that when you first hear them you do not know who is speaking and who is silent. So great is their similarity that it seems as if the same voice issued from both of them, and you may well repeat with Dante,

> Queste parole da lor ci fur porte.
> Da che io intesi quelle anime offense . . . .

> These words were borne to us from them. Soon as I had
> heard those injured souls . . . .—*Hell,* v, 108–9.

Why did the poet make these two hearts inseparable? Why did he make the two into one? Why, with hope dead, did love still live on?

Through a sublime inconsequence of Dante, answers my friend Dall'Ongaro, thus avoiding the difficulty. For his part, Foscolo tells of some sort of sympathetic concern the Poet felt for Francesca's family. Ginguené adds that "these two who go together" are not really damned; that they were guilty of no sin but a mere peccadillo, being killed before their desire achieved fulfillment; that Dante leaves the sin in shadow while giving sharp relief to the kind and lovable qualities of Francesca. Thus the best minds fall into sophistries when they seek the explanation in details rather than in the whole.

Those two who go together, love through all eternity not because they are not damned, but precisely because they *are* damned. In Paradise the earthly is raised up to the divine, whereas in Hell the earthly remains eternal and unaltered. In Dante's Hell the sinners retain all their passions, and are therefore impenitent and damned: Filippo Argenti is as irascible in Hell as he was on earth, Capaneus blasphemes in Hell as he did on earth. The mark of the damned soul is that he brings to Hell all his qualities and passions, good and bad; wherefore Francesca loved, loves, shall love, and can never cease to love. That is why the unhappy woman cannot tear this Paolo from her heart and has him always before her eyes—a sentiment the Poet represents concretely by placing her Paolo eternally at her side. This conception flashed through the mind of Silvio Pellico in one of the most felicitous passages of his tragedy, where, inspired by Dante, he has the dying victims utter these final words:

Francesca.   . . . Eterno
  Martir . . . sotterra . . . oimé . . . ne aspetta!
Paolo.   Eterno
  Fia il nostro amore.
Eternal torment . . . below . . . alas awaits us!—Eternal
  shall our love be.[24]

Eternity of love, eternity of torment. As if the poet wished to cast the sin in the shade! To say this is to separate what is indivisible; there is not the slightest detail here on which "sin" is not clearly stamped. In the first part of her tale Francesca left an immense gap: between her enamorment and her death lay a whole story, a story of love and sin before which the modest woman paused and fell silent. Dante lowered his head and re-

24. *Francesca da Rimini*, Act V, Scene 4.

mained absorbed, until Virgil asked him, "Che pense?" [What art thou thinking?] Dante could not reply immediately; when he finally did, he answered as if in a dream, speaking to himself, and could not address Francesca without weeping. What was on Dante's mind all that time? It was, of course, all this story of love and sin that he visualized.

Sin is the supreme pathos of this tragedy because the conflict which it engenders is not external to the lovers, but takes place in their very souls—and without conflict, love is not tragedy but Arcadian prose, pastoral poetry, Daphnis and Chloe. When the conflict arises because of accidental obstacles like differences in social station, family feuds, political hatreds, then the lovers, conscious of being right, can fight against obstacles existing outside their consciences. Not so with sin which, like love, is an infinite quality; the two coexist in the soul and one can never destroy the other; destroy the consciousness of her sin and you have destroyed Francesca da Rimini.

Francesca's struggle is endless, for she cannot say, "I love," without a voice answering, "It is sinful," nor can she hear that voice speaking to her, without at the same time conjuring back to her ever-constant mind the ill-repressed image. And what happens then? In the presence of others she studies her every word or glance, she strives to conceal the secret of her heart from herself as well as from others; but in the silence of her room, in the secret places of her heart she caresses that image, savors the sweetness of those thoughts, and nurtures those desires, until suddenly and all unaware she reaches the "dolorous pass," the moment of oblivion and guilt:

> Quanti dolci pensier, quanto disio
> Menò costoro al doloroso passo!

How many sweet thoughts, how great desire, led these unto the woeful pass!—*Hell,* v, 113–14.

This is the tragic background of the story, the divine tragedy which does not pass Francesca's lips, and which Dante's reverie, so touchingly portrayed, discloses and dramatizes. And what other meaning could the words of Francesca have in this story, if sin were omitted?

Soli eravamo e senza alcun sospetto.

We were alone and without any suspicion.—*Hell*, v, 129.

Who would ever make this remark except guilty love? They are reading together a love story but dare not look at each other, for fear that their eyes may betray what they know of, but conceal from, each other. When they come to passages in their reading that remind them of their own state, a common impulse with irresistible violence "urges" their glances, forces their eyes to meet. Forgetful, they raise their eyes, but lower them again, not daring to bear each other's gaze; and the consciousness of having betrayed their secret, and the thrill of the flesh, are revealed by the pallor on their faces:

Per più fiate gli occhi ci sospinse
    Quella lettura, e scolorocci il viso.

Many times that reading urged our eyes, and took the color
    from our faces.—*Hell*, v, 130–31.

"Per più fiate" [many times]. The struggle is repeated: they resist, forget themselves, resist anew,

Ma solo un punto fu quel che ci vinse.

But only one point was it that overcame us.—*Hell*, v, 132.

But this is not the truth; Francesca is deceived by a natural and lifelike illusion. They were overcome little by little. Paolo yields when to his inflamed imagination appears the desired object, the "object of dreams and sighs," which is not her lips, or even her smiling lips, as commentators explain, but the smile itself which is the expression, the poetry, the sentiment of the lips—something incorporeal which one sees hovering on the lips as if detached from them, and which you can see but cannot touch.

When Francesca is overcome and the sin that was already in
her soul stands revealed, then, at the very moment of the kiss and
even before she confesses her sin, Hell opens between *this one*
and *kissed my mouth,* between the lover and the sin. The "happy
time" is united with "misery," and that moment of abandon, her
sin, becomes ineradicable, becomes eternity!

> Questi, *che mai da me non fia diviso,*
> La bocca mi baciò . . . .
>
> This one, who never shall be divided from me, kissed my
>   mouth. . . .—*Hell,* v, 135–36.

What is all this? Is it joy? Is it sorrow? It is joy and it is sorrow,
it is love and sin, earth and hell, the bitterness of that love whose
wage is hell, the thrill of that hell where love still abides. It is a
complex emotion that defies expression. It is a living contradiction, the heart in all its mysteries, life in its contrasts, it is heaven
and hell, angel and demon; it is man.

This tragedy, developed in its basic outline and pregnant with
silence and mystery, has for its muse Pity, pure of any other
sentiment, a single and irresistible cord that thrills one's soul to
ecstasy. And this muse is Dante, already deeply moved as the
canto begins, and employing the most delicate images as if to
set the stage for the drama; Dante who, hearing the names of
ancient knights and ladies, is overcome with pity and "quasi
smarrito" [well-nigh bewildered—*Hell,* v, 72]; who is already
impressed by the mere sight of those two "that go together"; who
finds to portray them such a delicate comparison charged with
such graceful images; who, at the first words of Francesca, stands
absorbed in a vision full of sweet sadness, which he shakes off
reluctantly, with tears in his eyes; and who, at the end, "falls
like a dead body"—the final impression being made on him
not by the woman's speech but by the man's weeping. In this
slow crescendo of pity is it necessary to seek a "why"? Why
should Dante have to remember a similar sin committed by
himself? Doesn't this crude explanation reveal a cloistered man,

alien to all human affections, and accustomed to the recital of sins in the confessional? Dante is the echo, the chorus, the impression, the living man in the realm of the dead, bringing to it a human heart and making profoundly human the poetry of the superhuman.

The entire conception stands so firm and alive before the imagination that you cannot find here the slightest disharmony, the least trace of coldness. Virgil is superfluous in this trilogy, and he fades into the background, never betraying his presence. The whole composition seems to have been conceived in one breath, written down at one sitting, so great is the harmony and the technical perfection, down to the smallest detail. The verse itself yields to the overpowering will and responds with the sweet softness of its music to the most delicate intentions of the Poet.

The word that best expresses this perfection is genius. It is the genius that creates and informs, that bestows on everything about it something of its own life, with the ease and sprightliness of one at play.

In this genial creation are found the seeds of the finest creations of modern poetry, having at their center woman as released from metaphysics and mysticism and understood as a living person.

When I think of Silvio Pellico I cannot understand how so many nuances, such great refinement and delicacy of feeling, can have escaped him, and how from his pen could come a Francesca so monolithic, so crudely molded. I reflect further that Italian poetry has been generally unsuccessful in portraying woman, and that Francesca remains a solitary example. From so many lyrics not a single living woman has issued. In Ariosto, you are touched by the sweet laments of Olympia and Isabella,[25] but these are superficial sketches rather than serious portraits. In Tasso, Armida is overdone, Sofronia an abstraction, Erminia

25. Characters in Ariosto's *Orlando Furioso* (see in particular x, 27–34, and xxiv, 80–86).

insignificant, Clorinda reserved and cold.[26] Raphael's women live on the canvas, but you seek in vain any vestige of them in our poetry. We have "fading" women, women in whom life flashes at the very moment it is quenched, and who come to life at the moment of death, like Clorinda and Ermengarda. Leopardi's women, such as Sylvia or Nerina,[27] are embryonic creatures who disappear even before they taste life and love. Beyond these few fleeting creatures, vague wavering idealizations alien to reality, we look in vain for a real woman. No woman has survived in the work of Alfieri. Manzoni himself, powerful creator of individuals as he is, put something artificial and antiquated in his Lucia.[28] Occasional divine gleams of womanhood flash in Beatrice and Laura, but they lack sunlight. If we wish to find anything comparable to Francesca we must seek it in Shakespeare, Byron, Goethe, in foreign literatures, where we find women patterned after this first and immortal type—Francesca.

26. Characters in Tasso's *Gerusalemme Liberata:* Armida, iv, 28–33; xx, 128–36, and *passim;* Sofronia, ii, 14–54; Erminia, vi, 55–vii, 22, etc.; Clorinda, especially in xii, 2–69.

27. From Leopardi's *Canti:* Sylvia, in "A Silvia"; Nerina, in "Le Ricordanze."

28. The heroine of Manzoni's *I Promessi Sposi.*

IV

Farinata

BEFORE this colossal conception I pause and ask myself, "What was in Dante's mind when he conceived this image? [29] What feelings, what opinions affected him and set his imagination afire?"

The old generation, in going to its reward, leaves behind fresh memories that are like a family heritage. The old surviving actors of the play on which the curtain has just fallen, go about relating them to their children and grandchildren with the eternal refrain, "I was there!" In their stories they mingle the passions of the day with passions already dead, but still alive in their souls; and they exaggerate, alter, praise, vituperate —that is to say, they idealize—everything. This is the first history, or rather the first poetry, that makes a profound impression on the new generation. The French Revolution reached our ears even before we read about it in books; in the tales told by our fathers, Robespierre and the Jacobins rose before us rather like those frightful ghosts with which nursemaids people our childish imaginations, and Napoleon's adventures seemed a page from the Arabian Nights. These are the first impressions that inspire our

29. First published as "Il Farinata di Dante" in *Nuova Antologia* for May, 1869, then in *Nuovi saggi critici* (1873). Based on Lessons XXI and XXII of the first year's course at Turin.

youth. The secret charm of Béranger's poems, to mention just one example, lies precisely in the fact that Napoleon is represented in them as he lives in the tradition of the French soldier and peasant, not as he was in historical fact.

Dante's time was preceded by a similar period, made remarkable by the successive rise and fall of the Ghibelline party, and by a certain number of great men famous for valor and resourcefulness—Farinata, Cavalcante Cavalcanti, Jacopo Rusticucci, Tegghiajo, and others. The impression made on Dante by these great names, still living on in popular tradition, can be seen at the very beginning of the poem. When, taking his first steps in Hell, he meets an insignificant fellow named Ciacco, what is his first question? It is for news of these others, and their whereabouts:

> Farinata e il Tegghiajo, che fur sì degni,
>   Jacopo Rusticucci, Arrigo e il Mosca,
>   E gli altri, che a ben far poser gl'ingegni,
> Dimmi, ove sono, e fa ch'io li conosca.

> Farinata and Tegghiaio who were so worthy, Jacopo Rusti-
>   cucci, Arrigo, and Mosca, and the others who set their
>   minds on well-doing, tell me where they are, and make
>   me to know of them.—*Hell,* vi, 79–82.

The first on this list, and the greatest, is Farinata; and Farinata is the first one we meet.

One who reads the story of Farinata and of those times cannot avoid a feeling close to terror; such violence in passion, such obduracy in hatred make those ironclad men seem little better than wild beasts. But the history that presents them in this manner is a real mutilation, because it shows but one side of life. If we turn our gaze away from the public squares to look within domestic walls and private assemblages, then the Fredericks, the Enzos, the Manfreds, the Latinis, the Cavalcantis, who are so fiery in public contests, will be found discoursing peacefully of philosophy, holding courts of love, and writing sonnets and

ballads which are still rather crude, it is true, but reveal nevertheless a sincere and noble heart.

In one of these peaceful gatherings of the Muses, devoted to
disputations, to poetizing, to solving riddles and proposing
questions, an anonymous sonnet was one day read, addressed to
the four outstanding poets of the time: Guido Guinicelli, Guido
Cavalcanti, Dante da Majano, and Cino da Pistoja.[30] The sonnet
was set in a conventional mold, that is, the allegorical form
fashionable at the time, and it described an enigmatic dream
whose explanation was requested.

This was the sonnet:

A ciascun'alma presa e gentil core,
   Nel cui cospetto viene il dir presente,
   A ciò che mi riscrivan suo parvente,
   Salute in lor Signor, cioè Amore.
Già eran quasi ch'atterzate l'ore
   Del tempo che la stella è più lucente,
   Quando m'apparve Amor subitamente,
   Cui essenza membrar mi dà orrore.
Allegro me sembrava Amor, tenendo
   Mio core in mano, e nelle braccia avea
   Madonna, involta in un drappo dormendo.
Poi la svegliava, e d'esto core ardendo
   Lei paventosa umilmente pascea;
   Appresso gir lo ne vedea piangendo.

To every captive soul and gentle heart, into whose presence come the present rhymes, that they may write me
   back their opinion—Greeting in their lord, to wit, Love.
Already nigh a third of the hours of the time that every star
   is bright to us, had passed, when suddenly Love ap-

30. If the sonnet in question was indeed written, as Dante states in *Vita
Nuova*, III, on the occasion of his second meeting with Beatrice, when he was
eighteen years of age, it could have been sent neither to Guinicelli, eight years
dead, nor to Cino, aged then only fourteen. It was in fact sent to Cavalcanti, however, and the latter's sonnet in reply is extant.

peared to me, the memory of whose being maketh me shudder.

Gladsome Love seemed to me, holding my heart in his hand, and in his arms he had my lady, wrapped in a drapery and sleeping.

Then he awakened her and of this flaming heart, she fearful, did humbly eat: afterwards I beheld him go his way a-weeping.[31]

This sort of charade or *rebus* greatly pleased the gathering, and several of its members condescended to answer it, each interpreting the dream in his own way. Among these was Guido Cavalcanti, already famous as a poet, and a profound philosopher and moralist as well, who was striving to raise poetry to something substantial by wedding it to philosophy, and who scorned the bare poetic forms and poets like Virgil who employed them. Guido, then, must have been pleased with a sonnet conceived in accordance with his school and his style. He not only wrote an answer to it but sought to meet the author, feeling, with one of those impulses that reveal a noble heart, that he must be a young tyro just entering the poetical arena and concealing his name out of modesty or timidity. The author was a youth of nineteen, named Dante Alighieri. This was the beginning of a communion of feeling between Dante and Guido broken only by death. Both were high-minded, both poets, both in love; Dante would speak to Guido of his Beatrice, and Guido to Dante of his Mandetta. When they entered public life they were of the same party, both exiled, both unfortunate. When Dante lost his Beatrice, Guido wrote to him,

> Io vegno il giorno a te infinite volte,
> E trovoti pensar troppo vilmente:
> Molto mi duol de la gentil tua mente
> E d'assai tue virtù che ti son tolte.

> I daily come to thee uncounting times,

31. *Vita Nuova,* III.

And find thee ever thinking over vilely:
Much doth it grieve me that thy noble mind
And virtue's plenitude are stripped from thee.[32]

And Dante, in one of his moods of fancy and melancholy, wrote
to Guido,

Guido, vorrei che tu e Lapo [33] ed io
    Fossimo presi per incantamento,
    E messi in un vascel, ch'ad ogni vento
    Per mare andasse a voler vostro e mio;
Sicchè fortuna od altro tempo rio
    Non ci potesse dare impedimento;
    Anzi, vivendo sempre in un talento,
    Di star insieme crescesse il disio.

Guido, I would that thou and Lapo and I were taken by
    enchantment, and put in a vessel, that with every wind
    might sail to your will and mine;
so that tempest, or other ill weather could give us no hin-
    drance, rather, living ever in one mind, our desire might
    wax to abide together.[34]

This last line has a singular energy. Perhaps there is no one
who has not sometime dreamed thus, yielding to vain fancies,
turning his back on the wicked world and seeking refuge on some
deserted island, alone with his love or with his dearest friends.
And among Dante's dearest friends the closest and first was
Guido, as he says in the *Vita Nuova*.[35]

Such were the sentiments, the impressions of Dante's youth.
The preceding generation stood before him in its great men, of
whom he spoke with great affection and admiration. When he
met Tegghiajo and Rusticucci, he said,

32. *Sonnets and Ballate,* translated by Ezra Pound (Boston, 1912), p. 47.
33. Lapo Gianni, another poet. (Author's note)
34. *Canzoniere,* "Guido, vorrei. . . . ," ll. 1–8.
35. *Vita Nuova,* III.

Di vostra terra sono; e sempre mai
  L'ovra di voi e gli onorati nomi
  Con affezion ritrassi ed ascoltai.

I am of your city; and I have always rehearsed and heard
  with affection your deeds and honored names.—*Hell,*
  xvi, 58–60.

"Ascoltai!" ["I listened!"] One feels here the fresh impressions
of the youth when he first gave ear to those names and those
deeds. And with what touching simplicity does he speak of Ser
Brunetto!

Che in la mente m'è fitta, ed or m'accora
  La cara e buona imagine paterna
  Di voi, quando nel mondo, ad ora ad ora
M'insegnavate come l'uom s'eterna.

For in my mind is fixed, and now fills my heart, the dear,
  good, paternal image of you, when in the world hour by
  hour you taught me how man makes himself eternal.—
  Hell, xv, 82–85.

His own generation was almost identical with the preceding in
its opinions, its prejudices, sentiments, political parties, its loves
and hatreds. The illustrious houses maintained their primacy,
with glorious sons reviving the greatness of their fathers: Farinata
degli Uberti and Cavalcante Cavalcanti were no more, but now
there were Lapo and Fazio degli Uberti, Guido Cavalcanti. The
two generations were part of a single story, fully alive and present to the mind of Dante's contemporaries.

Later we find these men involved in political struggles, as
obdurate as their fathers, persecutors and persecuted. Then comes
the time of misfortune and disillusion. Guido had hardly returned
to Florence, when he died of the illness contracted in the un-
healthy sojourn of Sarzana where he had been exiled; Dante went

wandering from city to city without even the hope of ever returning to his fatherland. In these years of sorrow, life must have assumed a quite different aspect from that of the fair and fascinating years just past. Taking a stand by himself, outside any party, Dante rose above friends and enemies, and his wrath and partisan injustice were tempered by a nobler sentiment—his patriotism.

Beside this active life in which Dante moved and participated with the variety and energy of feeling which is the birthright of strong natures, there was another life, that of the schools and of books, from which he could derive a different, indeed a totally contrasting image of man and of the world. Here the great man, the hero, was not Farinata, but St. Francis of Assisi. Greatness was placed in poverty, abstinence, obedience, humility; real action was prayer and contemplation; the perfect life was ecstasy, the aspiration to cut loose the bonds of the "human" and attain the "divine." The representation of the human or carnal state of man, of his purification and glorification, this sort of "spiritual comedy" of the soul,[36] is the very concept that informs the *Divine Comedy* and lies at the root of all the didactical and poetical works of the time. Dante, as everyone knows, is the human soul represented in these three stages of its story, and Beatrice is Grace or Faith that leads it on to salvation. In its pristine simplicity this concept was not an abstract or theological view, but was life and action—there was faith then, there were miracles, and there were saints! But as early as the time of Dante it already was no longer a simple *datum* of faith, but a *probatum,* a theological-philosophical concept, mingled with Platonic and Alexandrine elements, with pagan traditions and scholastic subtleties. Hence Dante, like Bea-

36. Title of an allegorical play of the Middle Ages which is a story of the soul, conceived in accordance with these ideas. Its aim is to show how man achieves the "wholeness" and perfection of his existence by adding Grace to nature and Faith to reason—which is the concept of the *Divine Comedy.* (Author's note) This play is discussed in detail in De Sanctis' *Storia della Letteratura Italiana,* Vol. i, Chap. v.

trice, is not an active but a contemplative personage; he is an allegorical being, he is man or the soul in the story of redemption. He is an idea, not a character.

But within this ascetic and theological Dante, issued from the schools and from books, there still lives the other Dante, as history depicts him and as we have described him above: the partisan, the patriot, the exile, the disdainful and revengeful Dante, utterly human and carnal, in sharp contrast with the symbolic Dante. From this duality is born the essential originality of the *Comedy,* where the most mystical and ascetic qualities are combined with the most earthly and human, giving us a picture of the life of the age in all its gradations and contradictions, from the most intellectual to the crudest, from the highest to the lowest social strata, from the quibbling of the schools to the quarrels of public life and the mysterious depths of private life.

To be sure, with such a great variety of factors not integrated together, this world is not well fused or synthesized, and there remains an abstract and pedantic substratum, refractory to all efforts of the creative imagination. Two irreconcilable worlds stand face to face: the feudal-theocratic world which makes a dogma of the annulment of personality, and the world of the free commune where personality is everything. The former is a lyrical and didactic world, where man is the saint who prays and contemplates, while the latter is an epico-dramatic world, where man is the hero who labors and struggles; in one, man is still involved in the dark night of Myth, and stands as a type, not as a distinct individual, while in the other he appears in full consciousness of himself; one is the philosophico-artistic reflection of the past, the other is the prelude to modern life and modern art.

And what a prelude! The profoundest and most original conceptions of Italian poetry belong to this world of freedom and conscience, drawn from life, from that vivid storehouse of reality in which Dante is not only a spectator but also a leading and impassioned actor. It is here, in this world, beside Ugolino, Pier delle Vigne, Brunetto Latini, Capaneus, Nicholas III, Guido da

Montefeltro, in the midst of this train of great figures, that there rises up the image of Farinata.

As from within mystical Beatrice sprang forth Francesca da Rimini, woman in the fullness of reality, so from within this allegorical Dante springs Farinata. The allegorical Dante, protagonist of the "spiritual comedy" in the theological journey "from flesh to spirit," the symbolic being—humanity or soul, not yet a man but rather a type than an individual, an idea than a character—is transformed into Farinata, the free and conscious man, endowed with will and power, a consummate and fully developed poetic personality, pure of any doctrinal or mystical element.

There was much of Farinata in Dante; hence his great admiration for the great civic leader. Two things Dante held in utmost scorn: what is weak and what is plebeian, Pope Celestine and Master Adam. His ideal, his concept of being alive, of being a man, of the virile, the heroic, was strength; not of course physical, but spiritual strength, what he calls "magnanimity," greatness of soul, that unconquerable power that holds personality high above nature, above Hell itself, above all obstacles and vicissitudes. This conception of the virile is Dante's Muse of the Sublime, in both its negative and positive aspects, as can be seen from the following phrases:

> Guarda e passa.

Do thou look and pass on.—*Hell*, III, 51.

> Sciaurati che mai non fur vivi.

Wretches, who never were alive.—*Hell*, III, 64.

> Voler ciò udire è bassa voglia.

The wish to hear this is a base wish.—*Hell*, XXX, 148.

> E per dolor non par lagrima spanda.

And seems not to shed a tear for pain.—*Hell*, XVIII, 84.

> L'esilio che m'è dato, onor mi tengo.

I . . . count as my glory the banishment wreaked on me.[37]

Alma sdegnosa,
Benedetta colei che in te s'incinse.

Indignant soul, blessed be she who bore thee!—*Hell,* VIII, 44–45.

E cortesia fu in lui esser villano.

And to be churlish to him was courtesy.—*Hell,* XXXIII, 150.

The same conception flashes out again in that wonderful description of the voyage of Ulysses, foreshadowing Columbus, at the moment when Ulysses tells his men:

Considerate la vostra semenza:
Fatti non foste a viver come bruti,
Ma per seguir virtute e conoscenza.

Consider your origin: ye were not made to live as brutes, but to pursue virtue and knowledge.—*Hell,* XXVI, 118–20.

And where he says of Brutus:

Vedi come si storce e non fa motto.

See how he writhes and says not a word.—*Hell,* XXXIV, 66.

This concept of strength is also the source of three lofty creations in the *Comedy:* the personification of Fortune, Capaneus, and Farinata. In Fortune force is not yet freedom, not yet man; it is nature or necessity, devoid of feeling and struggle and thus, amid the imprecations of men, it remains immutably blissful and serene:

Ma ella s'è beata, e ciò non ode:
Con le altre prime creature lieta
Volve sua sfera e beata si gode.

But she is blessed and hears this not: with the other Primal

---

37. *Canzoniere,* "Tre donne intorno al cor. . . . ," st. 5, l. 4.

Creatures, glad she turns her sphere, and blessed she rejoices.—*Hell,* VII, 94–96.

In Capaneus the concept is taken in reverse and by antithesis to Pope Celestine. In this pope and the likes of him there is lack of strength, absence of life, while Capaneus is the bully boasting of his strength, proud to be alive: "Qual io fui vivo, tal son morto" [Such as I was alive, such am I dead.—*Hell,* XIV, 51]. In this profound conception of Dante, force is not a means to attain any of those high ideals for which our seed is made, but stands on its own. If I may be allowed to speak in a rather German manner, Capaneus is subjective force, force devoid of content, without purpose or motivation and therefore arbitrary; force for force's sake.

The ancients represented this concept in the fable of the Giants who wished to scale the Heavens; Jupiter striking them down with his thunderbolts stands precisely for the law of nature that avenges itself and hurls them down. Prometheus is silent and serene in his torment, because Prometheus is already a man, a free and conscious force with his own ideas and purposes who even in defeat can feel superior to Nature and to Jove. Capaneus, however, is not yet really human, but is the offspring of the Giants, still a mere brutish natural force, who appears colossal without but is empty and feeble inside. Actually, if we just look at the outer shell, this image of strength takes on imposing proportions. Killed by Jove's thunderbolt, Capaneus does not admit defeat but on the contrary declares insolently, "Such as I was alive, such am I dead." And not satisfied with this, he tries to set his strength in even bolder relief:

> Se Giove stanchi il suo fabbro, da cui
>   Crucciato prese la folgore acuta,
>   Onde l'ultimo dì percosso fui;
> E s'egli stanchi gli altri a muta a muta,
>   In Mongibello alla fucina negra
>   Gridando: Buon Vulcano, ajuta, ajuta,

Sì com'ei fece alla pugna di Flegra,
E me saetti di tutta sua forza
Non ne potrebbe aver vendetta allegra.

Though Jove weary out his smith, from whom in wrath
he took the sharp thunderbolt wherewith on my last day
I was smitten, or though he weary out the others, turn
by turn, in Mongibello at the black forge, crying, "Good
Vulcan, help, help!" even as he did at the fight of
Phlegra, and hurl on me with all his might, he should
not have thereby glad vengeance.—*Hell*, xiv, 52–60.

Capaneus conceives Jove in his own image. He imagines Jove
to be plebeian and crude, a purely material force, thus unwittingly painting his own portrait and voicing his own condemna-
tion. This Jove of his is "in wrath" because Capaneus dares to
boast of being his equal or his superior, and to have "vengeance,"
strikes him with the "sharp thunderbolt." Yet Jove fails to crush
the pride of Capaneus, who remains in death as he was in life,
nor shall Jove ever succeed, no matter what he may do—hence
his impotence, his perpetual wrath, and his "not glad vengeance."
From the bottom of Hell, Capaneus defies and insults Jove as
he did in life, and to demonstrate even more clearly the god's
impotence in struggling against him, he offers a succession of
"efforts," with a marvelous *crescendo,* ending with the representation of the god in the ridiculous attitude of pleading with
good Vulcan, crying out, "Help, help!" recalling with bitter
derision the battle of Phlegra in which Jove had been attacked by
the Giants. And to this god, arrayed in all his power, armed with
all his weapons, what does Capaneus oppose? A simple *me:*

E me saetti di tutta sua forza.

And hurl on me with all his might.—*Hell*, xiv, 59.

Here is a representation of truly wonderful energy and harmony;
everything in it—word, phrase, cadence, construction, coloring,

tone, style, form—springs from the Poet's deep and immediate contemplation.

But all this is just the outer skin, the simulation, the appearance of that force against which Jove himself seems powerless. Real strength lies within, in the spirit, and is simple and calm, for it needs no such theatrical display and pomp to affirm itself and to make us believe in it. Capaneus lies "dispettoso e torto" [despiteful and twisted] under the fiery rain which seems powerless to tame him,

> Sì che la pioggia non par che 'l maturi,
> So that the rain seems not to ripen him . . . .—*Hell,* xiv, 48.

but the more he boasts and the more he strains to show his strength, the less he succeeds, for real strength is seen, not proved. Because his strength was purely material, when he was struck by the thunderbolt Capaneus became convinced that Jove was materially stronger than he. His moral feebleness, however, keeps him from acknowledging this fact to himself or to others, and his language therefore displays an ostentation of strength, an effort to make it credible to others and to belie his own conscience. The sentiment born of this contradiction between appearance and reality, between inner weakness or consciousness of defeat and the pretense of strength and victory, is spite or "rage," the impotent rebellion of the proud when beaten and humbled by one stronger than they are:

> O Capaneo, in ciò che non s'ammorza
> La tua superbia, se' tu più punito:
>   Nullo martirio, fuor che la tua rabbia,
>   Sarebbe al tuo furor dolor compito.

> O Capaneus, in that thy pride is not extinct, art thou the more punished; no torment save thine own rage would be a pain adequate to thy fury.—*Hell,* xiv, 63–66.

Jove's thunderbolt had struck not only his body but even his soul.

So far, we have not met with the virile, the manly, with the sort of force that is free and conscious. In Farinata, Man appears for the first time on the modern poetical horizon.

Farinata not only makes no boast of strength, he is not even conscious of being strong. The concept of pure strength devoid of any content and intent only on self-satisfaction is alien to his character. He does not know that he is strong. This alone he knows, that he loves his party with all the energy and power of his soul. In Farinata force is not an abstract and empty power, as in Capaneus, but it is power inseparably wedded to ideas, motives, and goals of which he is conscious and which guide his conduct. This is not necessarily physical strength and may indeed be found at times in a weak body; it is spiritual strength, it is what Dante calls "magnanimity," that moral greatness which imparts beauty to the features and aggrandizes even physical stature in our image of it—what we today call mettle, or *character*.

In its esthetic sense character is not this or that part of the soul, but it is personality in its entirety, the whole man; it is not will and power in the abstract, but their living force manifested in ideas, feelings, deeds, and their motives and purposes. It is what Dante calls "being alive," and what constitutes the individual, the free and conscious person. In Pope Celestine there is absence of character. In the personification of Fortune [*Hell,* vii, 78], character is found crystallized, as in nature. In Capaneus it is pure strength, but in potency not in act. In Farinata force is not a mere abstract thing existing for itself, it has become incarnate and you can feel it living in the intensity of his feelings, his beliefs, his deeds. And this is character; this is personality with its wealth of determinations, its freedom of movement, life and action. Thus man emerges from the vagueness of a symbol or a pure ideal, and becomes a character in a drama: an actor.

But so far this is but the merest bare concept of man, of the virile; now we want to witness the most magnificent spectacle that humanity can view: we want to see this concept acquire motion, come to life, take on flesh, become a *form*. And when we see it before us, completely realized, we can say, "Behold the man!"

Farinata, the great man of the preceding generation, has long been alive in Dante's imagination, is a character he has long cherished and admired. We have already observed that on meeting Ciacco, Dante asked, "Where is Farinata? Let me know him." When he reaches the circle of the Heretics, he glances around: he knows Farinata for an Epicurean and hopes to find him there; but instead of men he sees only uncovered tombs.

> La gente che per li sepolcri giace
>   Potrebbesi veder?
> The folk that are lying in the sepulchers, might they be
>   seen?—*Hell*, x, 7–8.

he asks Virgil—a seemingly general question, whose real sense lies not in what it expresses but in what it leaves understood, in what Dante's lips leave unsaid but his eyes have already revealed; and Virgil with a glance guesses it:

> . . . satisfatto sarai tosto,
> Ed al disio ancor che tu mi taci.
> . . . thou shalt soon be satisfied, and also as to the desire of
>   which thou art silent to me.—*Hell*, x, 17–18.

While Dante utters a reply, half apologetic, half obsequious, suddenly a voice issues from one of the sepulchers; Dante in a natural instinct of fright draws closer to Virgil, and Virgil cries,

> . . . Volgiti: che fai?
> Vedi là Farinata che s'è dritto:
> Dalla cintola in su tutto il vedrai.
> Turn thee: what art thou doing? See there Farinata who has
>   risen erect; all from the girdle upwards wilt thou see
>   him.—*Hell*, x, 31–33.

Farinata's unexpected appearance on the scene is so prepared that he already looms big in our imagination although as yet we have neither seen nor heard him. He is big because of the importance the Poet has given him and the high place he holds in his thought. From Virgil's words we visualize him as colossal even before we see him:

> Dalla cintola in su *tutto* il vedrai.
> All from the girdle upwards wilt thou see him.

You wished to see him: there he stands, all of him, before you!

"All!" Tasso, portraying Clorinda contemplated by her lover as she stands on a slope, says:

> Tutta, quant'ella è grande, era scoperta.
> All, as tall as she is, was she revealed.[38]

"All" in this case does not express size and adds not a whit to Clorinda's natural stature. Its meaning must be sought in the lover's imagination, before which Clorinda appears in *all* her beauty; none of her shapeliness is concealed, and the lover gazes on it, charmed, and forgets Argante who is challenging him to combat. Virgil's *all,* in a different situation, has quite a different meaning. The import of this *all* is in Dante's preconceived idea of Farinata, and it means, "You shall see him in all his greatness." It thus has the function of what in the plastic arts is called relief, namely, to transfigure reality and give it the size our imagination attributes to it. Because our imagination can only conceive the abstract or intellectual by giving it shape or body, moral greatness for us lends greatness to the body itself: just as the common people, those born poets, on hearing tales of conquerors, visualize them as giants. In poetry, as well as in painting, the study of illusion is most important. The artist can achieve it naturally if his imagination is so clear and warm that the image stands before him in its entirety, not as a mere ex-

38. *Gerusalemme Liberata,* v, 26.

teriorization but as an expression of what is within, as character. Such is the attitude in which Farinata is represented:

> Ed ei s'ergea col petto e colla fronte,
> Com'avesse l'inferno in gran dispitto.

And he was straightening himself up with breast and front as though he had Hell in great scorn.—*Hell,* x, 35–36.

Farinata stands with half his body concealed in the tomb, the chest and front alone remaining in view; and yet he appears to us as if towering above all the objects about him. This is another illusion, another relief, brought about by the word "s'ergea" [was straightening himself up]. What is the meaning of this "s'ergea"? On meeting a great man for the first time, I should instinctively feel myself becoming quite tiny, even if I were a giant and he a pygmy; and the greater he were to me, the tinier I should feel myself becoming. On the other hand, there are base fellows who proudly strut about with head high, but they may stretch as much as they like, they will always be small because greatness lies not in the real size but in our imagination. When Kléber, in the enthusiasm of victory, says to Napoleon, "General, you are great," our imagination visualizes Napoleon on a pedestal and the giant Kléber, with bowed head, at his feet. Kléber, with all his authority over the army, was eclipsed before Napoleon because Kléber was imposing by his size but Napoleon ruled with a glance; one spoke to the senses, the other bewitched the imagination. That "s'ergea," taken merely in the material sense, is ridiculous; it is sublime here because it gives not only the figure but also the character:

> Com'avesse l'inferno in gran dispitto.
> As though he had Hell in great scorn.

That "straightening up" gives you the concept of a greatness all the more conspicuous because less measurable; it is the rising, the soaring of Farinata's soul above all Hell. Thus, with a single

stroke of his chisel, Dante has hewn the statue of the Hero, and
stamped on your soul the impression of an almost infinite
strength and grandeur.

Hell does not stand here on its own, in its literal sense of the
death of the soul, because what is striking here is surely not
Farinata the sinner, Farinata as a heretic: the sin is mentioned
only to explain why Farinata and Cavalcanti should be found in
this circle. Before Farinata's moral greatness, before his rising
up, all the other figures become secondary, and Hell itself serves
only to cast his grandeur into relief. In our imagination Hell is
the base, the pedestal, on which Farinata rises. And as Hell disappears, so does the symbolic Dante. Dante here is not the
human soul in its pilgrimage through the three states of life, but
is a Dante in flesh and bones, a citizen of Florence who admires
the great citizen of the last generation and before such greatness
feels reduced to nothingness. Behold him finally in the presence
of the man he has so longed to see! His glance is *fastened* to
Farinata's glance; he stands there ecstatic, overwhelmed, not
knowing what to do next, and Virgil must shake him, push him
toward the other. "You wanted so keenly to see and to speak to
Farinata; approach, so that he may hear you: 'le parole tue sien
conte'" [let thy words be clear].

> Io avea già il mio viso nel suo fitto;
> > Ed ei s'ergea col petto e con la fronte,
> > Com'avesse l'inferno in gran dispitto,
> > E l'animose man del Duca e pronte
> > Mi pinser tra le sepolture a lui,
> > Dicendo: le parole tue sien conte.

> I had already fixed my face on his, and he was straightening
> > himself up with breast and front as though he had Hell
> > in great scorn. And the bold and ready hands of my
> > Leader pushed me among the sepulchers to him, saying:
> > "Let thy words be clear."—*Hell*, x, 34–39.

The group is perfect in harmony and design. Farinata is seen towering over Hell, and Dante at a distance, motionless, astonished, his face fixed on Farinata's.

While this magnificent "stage setting" arouses in one's soul a feeling of greatness and strength, Farinata's first words inspire sympathy and affection. On his fiery bed, enclosed in his tomb, his ear is struck by Tuscan speech from the lips of a living man, and he leaps to his feet:

> Vedi là Farinata che s'è dritto.

> See there Farinata who has risen erect.—*Hell,* x, 32.

A Tuscan citizen, the speech of his native soil, his own Florence, his dearest memories throng in his mind and soften his haughty nature, giving his request a gentle tone, the accent of a prayer. In this wave of tender sentiments all that is harsh and excessive in the partisan's passionate soul is cleansed and purified; he feels remorse, or something akin to it, for having perhaps been, as a party leader, "molestful" to his fatherland, to his "noble fatherland":

> O Tosco, che per la città del foco
> Vivo ten vai, così parlando onesto,
> Piacciati di ristare in questo loco.
> La tua loquela ti fa manifesto
> Di quella nobil patria natio,
> Alla qual forse fui troppo molesto.

> O Tuscan, who goest thy way alive through the city of fire, speaking thus modestly, may it please thee to stop in this place. Thy mode of speech makes manifest that thou art native of that noble fatherland to which perchance I was too molestful.—*Hell,* x, 22–27.

"Perchance!" Here are nuances and delicate touches of feeling which spring forth in a spontaneous and unpremeditated manner, evoked by circumstances which the mind, as it discovers them, suddenly sees in an unexpected light. The suddenness is expressed in that first abrupt rush of words, before we even know whence they come or from whom. If Farinata were to say, "I was molestful to my fatherland," he would be expressing an opinion already formed, weighed, and decided. But the idea comes to him now for the first time, under the sudden impulse of one of those powerful waves of feeling that lay a man's soul bare; and in obedience to this sudden urge of tenderness his lips utter a confession, in the hasty and provisional form of a new and impromptu judgment which no one has yet had time to examine. Leopardi used to say that there is nothing more poetical than "perchance." [39] And I should like to add: nothing is deeper, since it relates to the most fleeting and delicate emotions of the soul. "I was molestful" expresses an absolute and abstract judgment; "perchance 'I was molestful" expresses it as felt at this very moment, as emerging from the immediately present conditions and impressions that arouse it: it gives you the opinion, not in the abstract realm of the intellect, but in the living act.

Passions, even when they are excessive, never pervade a noble soul so utterly as not to leave intact in its deepest recesses something pure and lofty which, under the stimulus of some extraordinary impression, shoots forth suddenly, diffusing its light and sympathy over the whole personality. With his profound intuition of the human heart, Dante seems somehow to give an added purity and beauty to Farinata's character by this outburst of noble feeling amid the violence of his passions. The great citizen ennobles and absolves the partisan.

But all this lasts only a moment: when Farinata sees this man draw near, looks him over and fails to recognize him, he becomes almost disdainful, suspecting that he may perhaps belong to the opposing political party. He who shortly before felt remorse for having been "perhaps molestful" to his fatherland by

39. In a note to his own *canzone*, "Ad Angelo Mai." Cf. De Sanctis' further comments on the same subject in the essay on Ugolino.

his passions, is a moment later possessed again by these same passions. Nature resumes her sway and the partisan stands revealed in all his crudity. It is not enough for Dante to be a Tuscan; to enjoy Farinata's good grace he must needs be a Ghibelline. "Chi fur li maggior tui?" [Who were thy ancestors?] In those vigorous days the party was not merely a bond of opinion but a family heritage: like father, like son:

> Poscia ch'al piè della sua tomba fui
>> Guardommi un poco, e poi quasi sdegnoso
>> Mi dimandò: chi fur li maggior tui?
> Io ch'era d'ubbidir desideroso,
>> Non gliel celai, ma tutto gliel'apersi;
>> Ed ei levò le ciglia un poco in soso,
> Poi disse: Fieramente furo avversi
>> A me ed a' miei primi, ed a mia parte;
>> Ond'io per due fiate gli dispersi.

> When I was at the foot of his tomb, he looked at me a little, and then, as though disdainful, asked me, "Who were thy ancestors?" I, who was desirous to obey, concealed it not from him, but disclosed it all to him; whereon he raised up his brows a little, then said: "They were fiercely adverse to me and to my forefathers and to my party, so that at two times I scattered them."—*Hell,* x, 40–48.

The impression of these haughty words, accompanied by such resolute gestures, is irresistible. But what element of the whole is possessed of such enchantment as to explain such an impression? Is it perhaps that blunt question, "Who were thy ancestors?" Or that gesture, so expressive of proud vexation, of raising his brows? Or perhaps the union he makes of himself, his fore-fathers, and his party, as if they were all one soul and one passion? Or that verb—I scattered them—planted there at the end of the phrase, solitary and detached, recalling in its con-temptuous rapidity Caesar's *veni, vidi, vici?* The secret lies in all of this, or rather in the very heart of the conception, which the poet contrived to seize in a single glance and from which springs such marvelous clarity of style; in that mixture of passion and strength which is the salient feature of Farinata's character. From this comes the striking harmony between words and gestures that mutually explain each other: brief and precise gestures and the broken, brusque, imperative speech of the man of action and command. This is the sort of strength that in the very vehemence of passion manifests itself without fitful or exaggerated gestures, with the assurance that a serious man has when speaking of himself. Farinata appeared to us immense in stature; we now find him in his words and recognize him as superior to Hell.

Dante, as we have said, had much of Farinata in himself. This man, shrunk to insignificance before that great figure, ecstatic, eager to please, on hearing his family insulted—be it even a Farinata speaking—feels the blood of his forefathers boiling in his veins, and he too rises before us colossal, to the level of Farinata himself. At this point we find the commentators displaying their pettiness as, embarrassed, they debate whether Dante was Guelf or Ghibelline when Farinata addressed him, and suggest that if his ancestors were Guelf and he Ghibelline, he could properly rise on this occasion to the defense of the Guelf cause. Oh ye political commentators! Dante is here neither Guelf nor Ghibelline, he is a son, and there is nothing so touching as this Dante who, before an enemy trampling his family, forgets party and self, becomes his own father, and replies,

> S'ei fur cacciati, ei tornar d'ogni parte
> . . . . l'una e l'altra fiata;
> Ma i vostri non appreser ben quell'arte.

> If they were driven out, they returned from every side
> . . . . both the one and the other time, but yours have
> not learned well that art.—*Hell*, x, 49–51.

One feels here that the flame of wrath has risen to Dante's face and that his forefathers speak through his lips. Farinata had said, "I scattered them 'at two times' "—accenting these last words. Dante throws back that plural resolved into two singulars, "both the one and the other time," and adds that sarcasm of the last line where, in that "badly learned art" of returning to the fatherland, one feels a seriocomic tone which implies laughter in the speaker—but bitter laughter.

"Arte mal appresa" [badly learned art] is one of those expressions that remain fixed in one's mind and are never forgotten. The shaft is shot and Farinata is hit.

But during this rapid exchange of words, between thrust and retort, Cavalcanti, the father of Dante's friend and companion Guido, rises from the tomb.

Farinata had asked, "Who were thy ancestors?" Dante answers that he is Dante of the Alighieri. This name [40] which had aroused Farinata's wrath, awakens quite a different feeling in Guido's father who was lying by his side. He thinks: Dante and Guido are friends, companions, both of lofty mind; if Dante is here alive, perhaps I may see here also my son Guido;—and he rises on his knees to look about:

> D'intorno mi guardò, come talento
>   Avesse di veder s'altri era meco;
>   Ma poi che il sospecciar fu in tutto spento,
> Piangendo disse: Se per questo cieco
>   Carcere vai per altezza d'ingegno,
>   Mio figlio ov'è? e perchè non è teco?

> It looked round about me, as if it had desire to see if another
>   were with me, but when its expectancy was quite
>   spent, weeping it said: "If through this blind prison thou

40. The reader should note that while Dante states that he "concealed nothing" from Farinata, he does not name himself at this point in the text. The name Dante occurs but once, when spoken by Beatrice at the climax of the entire poem in *Purgatory*, xxx, 55. It should be noted also that the "arte mal appresa" referred to a few lines above is not taken from line 51 in the preceding quotation, but (with a minor change of construction) from line 77 when Farinata resumes the subject.

goest by reason of loftiness of genius, where is my son?
and why is he not with thee?"—*Hell,* x, 55–60.

In the contemporaries of Dante and Guido, who knew their
story well, these lines must have aroused a wealth of feeling, of
ideas and memories lost to us today. Dante himself must have felt
intense emotion as he wrote them, for though Guido was alive
in 1300, the date of the allegorical journey, he was dead at the
moment when Dante was writing. And Dante must also have
reflected that it was on his advice that Guido had been banished;
that if he contrived later to have him recalled to Florence, it was
too late, for Guido died a few days later of the disease contracted in exile; and that he himself—who would have thought
of that when, as a Prior, he banished his friend?—he himself was
an exile with no hope of return.

Of all these feelings and memories no trace remains. All this
has perished, because in a work of art only those elements of
historical truth survive which have become imprinted and
fixed in its form—all the rest is irremediably lost. Events, circumstances, dates, an historical commentary can explain, clarify,
or recall; but it can never revive feelings or impressions, all those
nuances and fleeting or intimate gradations in which art finds
its goal. No poetry ever reaches posterity in its entirety; part of it
dies nor can history ever hope to resurrect it. And why should
this surprise you? Can you revive your own yesterday? How many
impressions and feelings, after but a single day, have already
faded from your memory never to return! The poet is only
human; he lives in history amid the transitory and cannot conceive the eternal apart from the temporary. How much of the
poetry in the *Divine Comedy* has perished, how many words have
lost their freshness, phrases their color, allusions their meaning!
The word, unlike the chisel or the brush, cannot represent the
entire figure. The word is not addressed to the senses but to the
imagination, and it often achieves its effect with a single stroke,
with an *all,* with an *arose.* A phrase is prosaic when it leaves our

imagination inert and void; it is poetry when many accessory ideas crowd the mind of the artist who has conceived it, and the artist has the power to suggest a similar rush of ideas in the mind of the reader. If these ideas are personal, however, the communion of feeling between poet and reader is broken, because personal ideas are intransitive, do not pass on, are not transmitted, remain with the person and die with him.

Mio figlio ov'è? e perchè non è teco?

Where is my son? and why is he not with thee?

The interest of this line lies in many personal ideas related to those days and to those men; it was no doubt a touching line to their contemporaries but it leaves us cold and dumb. Yet the scene as a whole has come through the centuries and aroused the constant admiration of posterity, because in this case the personal ideas form the background and the antecedents of the poetic fact, the occasion and inspiration for it but not its matter or substance. The poetry here derives its value, its interest, and its accessory ideas from human nature, immortal and ever young, and it preserves thus its freshness even when the impressions, facts, and feelings that inspired the poet have vanished.

In reality, the interest of this episode lies in the various affections and emotions that harrow the mind of a father, be he Cavalcante or anyone else. Surely it is not a matter of indifference that the father is Cavalcante, the son Guido, the poet Dante, and Dante's guide Virgil, a poet scorned by Guido. Historical reality contributes here to the general effect and constitutes the accidental, the accessory, the *obbligato* that gives the artistic creation its finishing touch, the complete appearance of truth; and historical reality is also, in this case, the occasional source of inspiration which moved the poet and aroused his imagination. But what his imagination produced is a creation independent of any personal idea and any historical accident; rooted in the living depths of the human heart it remains fresh and young, although the original ideas and their accessories are dead.

What is this poetry, in the last analysis? It is a page from the human heart in its most delicate gradations. These gradations are expressed sensibly in three instantaneous and unpremeditated movements, which the poet ascribes to Cavalcante, to a father: at first he rises on his knees, then he stands on his feet, and finally he falls back supine; actions which correspond to the three states of his mind, first a desire mingled with incredulity, then a painful anxiety, and finally an infinite grief.

At first he rises on his knees. He cannot believe what his mind tells him to be so strange, and yet he believes it because it is what his heart desires. His first gesture is a "perchance," belief and unbelief together, a "sospettare" [suspecting], glancing round about; and when he seeks and fails to find Guido, he weeps seeing his great hope dashed. So far the situation is moving but serene, but an ambiguous word from Dante raises it to the level of grief and anguish. Misunderstandings easily arise when the speaker and the listener are in different frames of mind. When Dante mentions Virgil, and hints at Guido's scorn for the great poet who guides and instructs him, he can well use a verb in the past tense and say "had in disdain,"[41] because his imagination is completely absorbed in the recollection of his youthful days, of his first discussions with Guido in schools and

41. De Sanctis has now referred several times to this obscure and disputed passage without actually quoting it. The text is:

> Da me stesso non vegno,
> Colui ch'attende là, per qui mi mena,
> Forse *cui* Guido vostro ebbe a disdegno,
> [*Hell*, x, 61–63]

which can be translated literally as meaning "I come not by myself; he who awaits yonder is leading me through this realm, *whom* (or, *to her whom*) your Guido had perhaps in scorn." De Sanctis, as usual, takes no interest in the textual or philological problem of interpreting the syntax of *cui,* but bases his discussion on the interpretation which, if not perhaps the clearest or most satisfactory, is the one accepted by the numerical majority of commentators, taking *cui* to refer to Virgil with the meaning *whom.* In any case, as the critic points out, the essential is that Dante should be thinking of his *past* days with Guido and thus speak of him in the past tense.

literary cenacles. That past tense, however, reaches the paternal ears without the accessory ideas that explain it, and acquires the meaning, "Your son is dead." This sudden tiding is immediately followed by an impulse of anxiety in his mind to which corresponds an equally instantaneous movement of his body:

> Di subito drizzato gridò . . . .
>
> Suddenly straightening up, he cried . . . .—*Hell,* x, 67.

a line in which the rising up and the crying out are expressed as simultaneous, almost as a single action, and where that unusual accent on the ninth syllable—the ò of "gridò"—lingers in the ear like the echoing overtones of a musical chord, representing and depicting the grief and heartbreak in the voice. These lines, unusual for the presence of the stress on the seventh or the ninth syllable, are as a matter of fact called Dantean, and when composed deliberately are very striking. Tasso has a well-known line of this type:

> La vide, e la conobbe, e restò . . . .
>
> He saw her, and he knew her, and he stood . . . .[42]

Tidings of great joy or great sorrow are not given credence at first. You wish you had not heard, had not properly understood; you repeat the words and want the news repeated; you hope you have misunderstood and you disbelieve your own ears:

> . . . Come
> Dicesti: "Egli ebbe?" Non vive egli ancora?
> Non fere gli occhi suoi lo dolce lome?
>
> How didst thou say, "he had?" lives he not still? does not the
> sweet light strike his eyes?—*Hell,* x, 67–69.

This is not a rhetorical figure, as in Tasso's lines,

> Io vivo? io spiro ancora? e gli odiosi
> Rai miro ancor di questo infausto die?

---

42. *Gerusalemme Liberata,* xii, 67.

> Alive am I? do I breathe yet? and the hateful rays do I still
> see of this unhappy day? [43]

because Tancred knew very well that he was alive, and had no
need to ask himself the question three times. But in Cavalcante
the heartbreak is real, following the equivocal word and the
silence of Dante, who stood before him as if in a fit of distraction
and made no reply. Hence his insistence, his repeating the same
thing, finding expressions ever more vivid, until he touches at the
end the pinnacle of emotion. What is life for Cavalcante, lying
in the "blind prison" of the tomb? It is light, the sweet light,
denied him through eternity:

> Non fere gli occhi suoi lo dolce lome?
>
> Does not the sweet light strike his eyes?

At each question of the father, Dante remains silent as if
absorbed. Some other thought seems to be crossing his mind. He
was wondering, "Since the damned know the future, why are
they ignorant of the present? Why doesn't Cavalcante know
that Guido is still alive?" But for Cavalcante, Dante's silence had
a frightful meaning. That silence meant, "Your son is dead!"
There are moments when a word is like the stab of a dagger;
no one dares utter it, everyone stands silent and that silence is
more eloquent than an oration. When Achilles asked of Patroclus
and saw that everybody around was quiet, he exclaimed, "Patroclus is dead!"—"Your son is dead!" and Cavalcante, as if thunder-
struck, falls back supine:

> Supin ricadde, e più non parve fuora.
>
> He fell again supine, and appeared no more outside.—*Hell,*
> x, 72.

Sorrow is sublime when, at some unexpected news, the various
emotions cluster and crowd in sudden confusion within the
mind, overwhelm and prostrate it. To say that our sorrow was

43. *Ibid.,* 75.

inexpressible, ineffable, unspeakable; to say that tears failed our eyes, words our tongue, is to use commonplace phrases that have lost their efficacy. If you wish to give sublimity to the inexpressible, you must express it. If you wish to make size sublime, show me a Pyramid. If you wish to make sorrow sublime, cover with a veil the head of Agamemnon before Iphigenia's sacrifice, or describe a man falling suddenly "like a dead body"; and, above all, conceal it from my sight, for the less I see, the more I imagine. Of this nature is the sudden fall of Cavalcante, then the silence of the tomb, "and he appeared no more outside."

At this point we have more trivial questions from the commentators. Why did Dante interrupt Farinata's tale? Why did he intrude this episode which has nothing to do with it? And why was Farinata indifferent to such a pathetic scene? To mention one answer, here is Foscolo's. Searching through old chronicles, he discovered that Cavalcante's son was Farinata's son-in-law, and he concluded that this fact explained the relationship between the principal event and the episode. He further believed that Dante depicted Farinata as impassive before the news of his son-in-law's death in order to show that the public man must not feel private affections. Here we fall into a pitiful sort of *fabula docet*. Since when is it forbidden to a public man to shed tears on his private woes? Even when the sacrifice of private feelings is demanded, it is not weakness to feel emotion, but to yield to it. That sacrifice is nobler which costs the more tears, and if you wish to portray Brutus condemning his sons to death, you must show him in tears if you expect to arouse my interest. Before a sight so piteous Farinata "changes not his aspect, nor moves his neck, nor bends his side" [*Hell,* x, 74–75]. Why? Look at Berchet's Giulia[44] in the temple, amid a crowd of people in

44. *Giulia,* one of the *romanze* of Giovanni Berchet, is the story of a Lombard mother. Her elder son is in exile because of his opposition to the Austrian rule of his fatherland; her younger son has reached military age. While she awaits in church, with all the villagers, the drawing by lot of the names of the seven youths, she is haunted by the fear that if her son is drafted he may some day have to fight his own brother. His name is the last drawn.

various attitudes while she alone, motionless, hears nothing, sees nothing, "non guarda che in cielo" [but looks up to heaven]. Why does she seem estranged from this great swarm of things and people? Because Giulia is a mother; because her thoughts are all concentrated on her son, whom she fears to see chosen by lot to become an Austrian soldier with the eagle on his cap; because at that moment her son is her whole world. And why does Farinata, the magnanimous, remain motionless like a statue? Because he neither sees nor hears; because Cavalcante's words enter his ears but not his mind; because his mind is entirely concentrated on that single thought—"the badly learned art"—that pierced him through like an arrow, and whatever else takes place about him passes unnoticed. What are Farinata's first words after Cavalcante disappears?

> E se, continuando al primo detto,
>   Egli han quell'arte, disse, male appresa,
>   Ciò mi tormenta più che questo letto.
>
> "And if," he said, continuing his first discourse, "they have
>   ill learned that art, it torments me more than this bed."
>   —*Hell,* x, 76–78.

During all this time Farinata has been thinking only of what Dante said. Between those words of the poet and Farinata's reply is an interval occupied by Cavalcante which is an interruption for the reader, but for the "magnanimous" is a continuation of the same thought, a prolongation of the same grief. It is a grief that he wants to dominate alone, that bears no company, that leaves him indifferent to the death of his son-in-law and makes him indifferent to the very fire of Hell. Moral sorrow makes him forget his physical pain, or rather it reminds him of it only to show that by comparison his sorrow is even greater:

> Ciò mi tormenta più che questo letto.
>
> It torments me more than this bed.

Here we can see how far apart are the boastful vanity of Capaneus and the austere grandeur of Farinata. Capaneus speaks with insolence in order to conceal from himself and from others the consciousness of his own defeat. Farinata has nothing to conceal; every word comes straight from the heart and before Dante, who shot the arrow, he reveals the infinite depth of his suffering. But, as a proud man, he hurls back the arrow whence it came. "You say that mine have ill learned the art of returning to our fatherland; but you too shall learn by experience how difficult it is to learn that art." It is the very arrow shot by Dante that returns to pierce his own heart:

> Ma non cinquanta volte fia raccesa
> La faccia della donna che qui regge,
> Che tu saprai quanto quell'arte pesa.

> But the face of the Lady who rules here will not be rekindled fifty times ere thou shalt know how much that art weighs.—*Hell*, x, 79–81.

But in opening a wound in Dante's heart, Farinata feels no solace in his own and cannot resign himself to the thought that the people should be so "pitiless" toward his family. Dante reminds him, not without a touch of irony, of the battle of the Arbia where he *scattered* the Guelfs:

> . . . Lo strazio e 'l grande scempio
> Che fece l'Arbia colorata in rosso,
> Tale orazion fa far nel nostro tempio.

> The rout and the great carnage which colored the Arbia red cause such prayer to be made in our temple.—*Hell*, x, 85–87.

And now another trait springs out in this character so full and rich. If you look at a battle as a whole you are struck with admiration, but if you look at this or that dying soldier you are moved to tears. When Farinata says, "At two times *I* scattered them," his expression seems sublime because it shows a great man who, almost with a glance, puts his enemies to flight. But when Dante throws back in his face the bloodshed of his fellow citizens, and shows him the Arbia colored red, then the proud man sighs, and he who had just said *I,* cannot now bear alone the weight of such a reproof and seeks companions to share it. He soon raises his head again, however, finding the finest deed in all his life, a deed whose glory is all his, his alone; and the scene is pervaded with light and beauty: the bloody conqueror of the Arbia is succeeded by the savior of Florence in a final image which is the purification and the transfiguration of the partisan:

> Poi ch'ebbe sospirando il capo scosso,
>   A ciò non fu' io sol, disse; né certo
>   Senza cagion sarei con gli altri mosso:
> Ma fu' io sol colà, dove sofferto
>   Fu per ciascuno di tôr via Fiorenza,
>   Colui che la difese a viso aperto.

> After he had, sighing, shaken his head, "In that I was not alone," he said, "nor surely without cause would I have moved with the others; but I was alone there, where it was agreed by everyone to destroy Florence, he who defended her with open face.—*Hell,* x, 88–93.

The last line is an epigraph, the apotheosis, and it has for centuries been the typical motto that concludes and sums up the life of this Hero.

To be sure, the type of Farinata is still too simple for modern man; in him the human stuff is still epic, not yet dramatic. It has no eloquence, no inner spiritual life. A grand nature is there but, like Memnon's statue,[45] it needs the impact of external im-

---

45. One of the colossal statues of the Egyptian King Amenophis III, near Thebes, which, after its partial destruction by an earthquake, gave forth a musical sound when touched by the rays of the rising sun. This phenomenon was mentioned by Strabo, Pausanias, Juvenal, and Tacitus.

pressions to produce a sound. Those impressions are contrived with great felicity and originality, and yield wonderfully dramatic effects—what we would call today "colpi di scena" [sensational scenes]; that sound is a single, rapid emission, but it allows glimpses of all the depths of feeling underneath, though these depths are not developed or analyzed. Farinata is a type of man still primitive and spontaneous in his simplicity. Completely extroverted, without meditation or self-analysis, he leads a sort of synthetic inner life that awaits outer impressions before reacting with energy. That is why the expression is often found in a single trait. As you proceed, you no longer have before you the same sentiment, graded and restated, but a new impression and a new emotional reaction to it. This is perfectly in keeping with our Poet's manner of conception and expression; his characterizations are sketches rather than complete and rich representations. The character that is best developed and graded in a single representation is Ugolino, hence the poetry there is more modern and more popular.

Here sharply defined outlines are lacking. You have the essential traits, flashes of light that suddenly illumine (if I may be permitted the metaphor) the whole horizon of the inner life. And all these traits taken together reveal the deepest and most intimate features of what Dante conceives as the virile type, the man of the free commune, released from the symbolism of feudal and theocratic ages and rising to the highest levels of strength and moral grandeur, becoming a *character*.

It is a sad but obvious reflection for one who knows our history, that this man of Dante, the Farinata type—the stuff that Shakespeare's great characters are made of—is the one and only example of his type in our poetry! Dante himself, in his essential traits, seems a poet extraneous to Italian art! We show a rhetorical admiration for him but we are alien to his spirit.

Awakened after the long slumber of servitude, we replaced Dante on our altars, and both poets and prose writers strove to inject some of that blood, some of that vitality into the veins of

our people. They wanted to replace the Metastasio man—
rhetorician, singer, dancer, sonneteer, academician, and Arcadian
—with the Dante man, and more than one Diogenes went out in
search of him. There was constant talk of force and greatness, of
dignity and manhood. But Dante's man failed to appear, precisely because he was being sought; what appeared instead was
the arid and abstract man of Alfieri, found not in living society
but in the haughtiness of a solitary soul. Thus were born all these
types of Brutus, of Timoleon, of Agides or of Icilius,[46] who are
as remote from Farinata as the living presence of Dante's Italy is
remote from an Italy fashioned by individual thought and
christened "Italy of the future."

46. *Brutus, Timoleon,* and *Agide* are the titles of three of the tragedies of
Vittorio Alfieri; Icilius is a character in his *Virginia.*

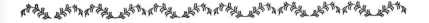

V

Pier delle Vigne

THE exceptional severity of this winter has kept me from beginning these lectures earlier.[47] Perhaps I should not have been
able to begin at all if some friends, mostly Piedmontese, had not
smoothed the way by means of a subscription. Allow me, gentlemen, to offer my thanks publicly to these kind friends, especially
as their intention goes beyond my person. Each century has its
beloved, its favorite poet. There was an age of Petrarch, one of
Metastasio, one of Tasso; ours is the age of Dante. Not long ago
the French came in throngs to applaud the lectures of Ozanam,
that fervent interpreter of Dante; Foscolo and Rossetti have
made the *Divine Comedy* so popular in England that I remember
seeing English tourists wandering about the hills of Sorrento
with Dante in their pockets, and English girls, seated near
some statue or fountain in the public gardens of Naples, absorbed in their vest-pocket Dante, contemplating pensive
Mathildas or Beatrices. Just now, perhaps on the very day I am
addressing you, Göschel in Berlin is explaining the *Divine
Comedy* to a numerous public, in the presence of an August

47. This is of special interest as being a reproduction, only slightly modified
for publication, of the opening lecture in the second year's course at Turin in
1855. It is thus the earliest in date of all the Dante essays and the most polemical
in tone. It was published in *Lo Spettatore* (Firenze, anno I, no. 33, 8 luglio 1855),
and revised to enter the *Saggi critici* in 1866.

Personage,[48] and perhaps today our own Dall'Ongaro in Brussels is stirring up Belgian enthusiasm for Dante. Gentlemen, what for foreigners is a literary admiration, is for us something more —a sacred duty. Since Fate denies us at present the accomplishment of great deeds, my kind friends wish us to prepare for what we may some day be, by learning from our great ancestors what we once were, especially from a poet who loved his country so much and made it so great. As for me, I shall not speak of my limited talents nor of the paucity of my studies in a perfunctory display of modesty that would no longer be believed. I shall merely say that I do not consider myself unworthy of your benevolence, because I prepare these lectures with loving care, sparing myself no effort; because they are for me a constant preoccupation, the object of daily meditation.

How shall I begin? Shall I read you an introduction, an inaugural dissertation as they are called? I forbore doing so last year, nor shall I do so now. Inaugural dissertations had their meanings once; now they are mostly conventional discourses, empty ceremony. Cold and insipid like all ceremonial speeches, they are a kind of antechamber in which the public is detained before being admitted to the business at hand. I wish to spare you this waiting room. And I will spare you also the summary of previous lectures, since we have now reached a point where we can undertake the explanation of the single cantos of *Hell*, referring only occasionally and briefly to certain fundamental principles.

In the three Dantean worlds, I have shown you our own world emended and refashioned according to conscience, such as we sometimes conceive it when, before a crime rewarded, before some reality that clashes utterly with our conception of a moral order, we burst out with the bitter exclamation, "And yet the world should not go that way!" This *should* is the meaning of the

---

48. In 1853 Karl F. Goeschel delivered a course of lectures on Dante before the Evangelical Association of Berlin, in the presence of the King of Prussia, the "August Personage."

Dantean world. It is reality corrected, the world straightened out with everything in its place. *Hell* is one of the facets of the world: it is the society of the evildoers, the realm of evil, of error, of ugliness, the story of human sins, and not of sins thrown together at random: for there is not only succession but connection, not only movement but progression; and progress in Hell is regression, a constant regression from human to bestial, from spirit to flesh. I have already shown you all this in the nature of the place, in the penalties, the demons, the groups, the damned—Incontinent, Violent, and Frauds.

In the first two classes of damned, evil does not proceed from vice, malice, or cold premeditation, as it does in the Frauds and Traitors. Evil proceeds instead from impulse of passion, from violence of character, and that passion awakens our pity, that character arouses our admiration. I wish to close this series of great poetical characters I discussed with you last year, by speaking today on Pier delle Vigne, or on the canto of the suicides.

I open some commentaries: Costa, Colombo, Cesari go into ecstasies before the "stizzo verde" [green brand], the "cigolare" [hissing], the "divellere" [tearing itself], and the "balestrare" [flinging], admiring, and rightly so, the propriety and vivacity of the words employed; these are grammatical commentaries. I open some more commentaries: Biagioli and others like him point out the passages imitated from Virgil, the imitative harmony of "cigola per vento che va via" [hisses with the wind that is escaping] and the antithesis "non frondi verdi, ma di color fosco" [not green foliage but of color dusky], etc.; these are rhetorical commentaries. What is the value of these commentaries? I find in some writer the phrase, "face suffused with color," and I forthwith jot down in my notebook the phrase, "face suffused with color." What am I doing? I am scraping the color from the face of a Madonna by Raphael to cast it back on the palette; I am destroying animate matter to make it again into raw material. I am like the barbarian who broke up the masterpieces of Greek sculpture, the statues of Corinth which he did not understand, to get from them the one thing he could understand, marble. That color, gentlemen, which lies as a lifeless phrase in my notebook, is indignation on the pale face of Father Cristoforo in the presence of Don Rodrigo offering his protection to Lucia; [49] that color is modesty on the cheeks of Juliet, blushing at the passionate words of Romeo; that color is mere pigmentation, when it lies as mere stupid matter on the shameless face of Domitian: on his red face no shame appeared, in the sublime phrase of Tacitus.[50]

I turn to other commentaries. Marchetti & Co. speak of Pier delle Vigne, of Guelfs and Ghibellines, of Papacy and Empire: they fall into the same error as the above commentators by recounting facts and incidents apart from the characters and passions which alone can explain the story that Dante raised to poetry; they give us a vocabulary of dates and events instead of a vocabulary of phrases. I open other commentaries: Boccaccio [51] maintains that the Harpies stand for avarice. Not at all, exclaims another; the Harpies stand for rapacity and violence. You are wrong, affirm Rossetti and Aroux; the Harpies are the Dominican monks. Are you laughing, gentlemen? And does not Dante say, remarks Aroux, "human necks and faces?" He speaks of animals but he means men. And does he not add, "feet with claws," which perfectly represent the rapacity of those monks? And what is that "pennuto il gran ventre" [the large belly feathered—*Hell,* XII, 14] if not a large belly, the large belly of the Dominicans?

Gentlemen, commentaries of these kinds—grammatical, rhetorical, historical, allegorical—are inadmissible nowadays. Without condemning commentators or their commentaries, which represent their own age, I say that they are no longer admissible because for the past half-century the science of criticism has been

49. Characters in Manzoni's *I Promessi Sposi.*

50. Tacitus, *Vita Agricolae,* 45: "saevus ille vultus et rubor, quo se contra pudorem muniebat."

51. Boccaccio is the author of the first biography of Dante and of a commentary on the first sixteen cantos of *Hell.*

proceeding on a new path, and after putting up a brief struggle the old criticism no longer opposes its principles to the new. But while the scientific struggle is over, the old criticism still persists in practice. It still persists because of the force of inertia, habit, tradition, because of that sort of passive, plebeian resistance that so hampers the triumph of truth, be it intellectual or social. Science has taken not merely different, but even opposite paths, as usually happens: it has run to the other extreme. It seems to say, "You give us phrases, and I give you concepts; you give us historical facts, and I give you historical laws."

Risen in Germany, diffused throughout France, this new science has had Vincenzo Gioberti as its most illustrious representative among us. This is how it puts the fundamental problem of esthetics: what is the concept and what is its historical form, that is, how did it develop in this or that century? The German school deals preferably with the concept, and its criticism reads like a dissertation; the French school finds more satisfaction in lingering over the historical form, and its criticism resembles a narrative. I say schools advisedly because I do not refer to individual critics, some of whom are gifted with the greatest talent—and talent possesses some sort of clear intuition of truth that keeps it outside of systems and raises it above schools. But even as great poets are succeeded by poetic schools, so great critics are succeeded by critical schools where the vitalizing genius is missing and only the tendency and the system remain.

The German school is dominated by metaphysics; the French, by history. Is Opitz [Kopisch] to speak on Dante? Then he will discuss Love, Grace, Woman in the Middle Ages, and so on—a path Dall'Ongaro seems to have followed, from what I can gather from the brief newspaper accounts of his lectures. He has divided the *Divine Comedy* into single concepts—Papacy, Empire, woman, religion, monastic orders, philosophical doctrine, economic doctrine, etc.—and is devoting a lecture to each of them. If this be the case I must say, begging Signor Dall'Ongaro's pardon, that he is replacing a vocabulary of words by a vocabulary of concepts—the type of criticism in which you immediately recognize the German school at its worst. The French school is dominated by history. Is Nettement to speak on Delavigne, Barbier, Victor Hugo? Then he will give you the history of Louis Philippe, of the opinions and passions in vogue at that time; by these historical promenades you can recognize the French school. I wish to offer you, gentlemen, a sample of criticism in the French and the German manner. As a basis for criticism it is too general, but still it is a basis, and by testing it we shall better be able to see its weak side. In other words, in discussing the canto of the suicides, I propose to begin with these questions: What is the concept of suicide? What is its historical form?

Suicide was the last virtue of the ancients. Amid the complete disintegration of every moral principle and every belief, the ancients formulated under the name of Stoicism a philosophy of death: since they no longer knew how to live heroically, they wanted to learn how to die like heroes. The type of the ancient suicide is Cato, its poet Lucan, its historian Tacitus. Tacitus' solemn melancholy is heart-breaking: having no great deeds to relate, he takes a sad pleasure in relating great deaths as the last remaining vestige of Roman greatness. At almost every page you meet with a new suicide—the only freedom Tiberius left to the Romans, the freedom to die.

The extent to which Christianity modified ancient science and morals, and therefore art, can be inferred from this alone: ancient suicide was a virtue, modern suicide is a crime; the pagan suicide was a hero, the Christian suicide is a coward. Whence does this historical difference arise? Here the French critic yields and the German takes the floor. It arises from the diversity of concept. To the ancients a free man was one who knew how to die. Liberty was not an abstraction but something concrete and actual, and when he met with insuperable obstacles that would impair his freedom and his human dignity, he took his own life to maintain his freedom. And this not because he considered life despicable and wearisome, for, on the contrary, it was always Heaven's dearest gift; but liberty to him was even dearer:

> Libertà va cercando ch'è sì cara
> Come sa chi per lei vita rifiuta.

> He goes seeking liberty, which is so dear, as he knows who for it renounces life.—*Purgatory,* I, 71–72.

Cato could live only as a free man, and when liberty died, Cato died. This firm, almost fierce disposition, this assurance of constantly carrying his own liberty in a ring on his finger, constitutes the moral greatness of the ancient suicide and makes him sublime.

> Morire innanzi che servir sostenne.

> He preferred to bear death rather than slavery.[52]

In Christian spiritualism the concept is different. Freedom is in the soul; not outside, but within us; man is free even in a prison because his soul is free. Hannibal killed himself to avoid falling into the hands of the Romans; the Christian holds his head high even behind the triumphal chariot of the conqueror because his freedom is within himself, not in the hands of fortune or of men. Hence that serene resignation which is the hallmark of the Christian hero, and of which Silvio Pellico offered us a rare example. Christian freedom consists in the restraint of sensuality, in resistance to the passions, in maintaining equanimity in every vicissitude. Of this I would consider Napoleon an exemplar, when he condemned Cato and chose to live through a long agony at Saint Helena, if his *Memoirs* did not betray something bitter and spiteful, the language of the vanquished. His greatness needed more serenity in good fortune and more simplicity in misfortune.[53] If, therefore, man yields to

52. Petrarch, *I Trionfi,* II, 60. Correct reading is "Morir in prima che servir sostenne."

53. Lively approbation. (Author's note) It will be recalled that we are reading the text of a lecture, given at a time when the government of Piedmont (capital,

fortune; if, his life having grown wearisome to him, he casts it away as an unbearable burden, depriving himself of something not his own; then you may call his action virtue, but it is sin— you may call it magnanimity but it is weakness.

Such is the simple theme on which a German would build a dissertation and a Frenchman a narrative; Saint-Marc Girardin [54] might intrepidly start with Sappho and come down to Werther and Jacopo Ortis.[55] Is this criticism? We have before us a very general concept, applicable to all forms of writing and expression —to eloquence, poetry, history, science, painting, sculpture, etc.; applicable to all the writers of one century or several centuries, to the great, the mediocre, and the insignificant. In vain we seek in this generality a content that is peculiar to poetry and peculiar to Dante. If you take a schoolboy's oration on the topic of suicide and cut out the amplifications, the figures of speech, and flowers of rhetoric, what will remain at bottom? The same concept. If you take a seminarian's dissertation on suicide, and delete the theological references, scriptural and other citations, and the other usual ingredients, what will remain at bottom? The same concept. Now, what sort of criticism is this, which makes no distinction between an oration and a dissertation, between a dissertation and a poem? What sort of criticism is it which sees no difference between Dante and a schoolboy or a seminarian? We cannot therefore avail ourselves of a basis that is so general, and must find a point of departure that is peculiar to poetry and to Dante.

The poet visualizes persons, not ideas, the criminal, not the

---

Turin) was preparing to enlist the help of Napoleon III for the liberation of northern Italy from Austrian domination.

54. De Sanctis is obviously referring to his most important work, the *Cours de littérature dramatique, ou de l'usage des passions dans le drame* (1843), where he compared the expression of passion in classical and modern literatures, stressing the superiority of the ancients. De Sanctis published an essay on the *Cours* a few months after the publication of the present study.

55. Protagonists of two epistolary novels ending with the suicide of the hero: Goethe's *Die Leiden des jungen Werthers*, and Foscolo's *Le ultime lettere di Jacopo Ortis*.

crime of suicide. What is Dante's *Hell?* It is the reproduction of the act of sin: that is, not nature as we see it, in its entirety, but only sinful nature in sinful act. Hence the Hell of the suicide is the individual suicide himself, viewed at the moment when he turns savagely on himself to separate violently what nature has joined. This separation against nature, which in life is the result of a single moment of blind passion, Dante makes eternal; this wound that the suicide inflicts upon himself, Dante makes eternal. The soul shall never reacquire the body from which it tore itself violently,

> Che non è giusto aver ciò ch'uom si toglie,
> For it is not just for one to have that of which he deprives
> himself.—*Hell,* xiii, 105.

and it shall remain enclosed within an extraneous body of a lower order, within a plant, with the plant feeling at all times the wound which the suicide opened in life:

> Le Arpie, pascendo poi delle sue foglie,
> Fanno dolore, ed al dolor finestra.
> The Harpies, feeding then upon its leaves, give pain, and to
> the pain a window.—*Hell,* xiii, 101–2.

The separation is eternal, the wound is eternal; the suicides' Hell is the act of self-destruction repeated eternally at every instant.

This is not the concept, but the conception, that is to say the concept embodied, made visible and accessible to the senses in a manner peculiar to poetry and to Dante. Now, before you form such a conception you are still free; but once any such conception whatever begins to take form in your imagination, you become subject to its inner laws: from the conception of a man you cannot draw an animal, without risking an abortion lacking any warmth or vital force. If you have talent, if you feel man enough to make your conception fertile and bring it to perfect life, you must accept the situation in which it puts you and the representation it demands.

And what is the situation with which it confronts you? That is to say, what are the esthetic laws, the conditions according to which the conception must develop and grow into life? Before you is a plant which holds a man's soul imprisoned within itself and moans, bleeds, and speaks. Now in esthetics anything that is outside natural law, such as a winged horse, a centaur, a talking plant, is called fantastic: fantasticality is therefore the first esthetic law of this conception. What is the emotion that springs therefrom? A suicide is not a hero, as in the pagan concept, but neither is he a scoundrel; he is a weak man, perhaps a good man, who is driven to self-destruction by grief and kills himself through impatience of suffering, because of "disdegnoso gusto" [scornful disgust—*Hell,* XIII, 70]; therefore he does not inspire repulsion or horror, but pity, profound pity! The situation then with respect to the imagination is fantastic, with respect to feeling is pathetic.

The situation determines the representation, whose only purpose must be to put into evidence and cast into relief those elements in the conception which are fantastic and pathetic, marvelous and affecting.

We find a thing fantastic if it is abnormal by our natural standards. Let us imagine that the Moon is inhabited by animated plants: to such creatures Dante's animated plants would certainly not be fantastic. The forest of the suicides is fantastic to us because it differs from our earthly forms, and the more this contrast is emphasized the greater is the marvel. In this lies the whole art of representation.

To achieve this Dante needs no remarks, exclamations, or apostrophes, grandiloquent phrases, claims to hair-raising or blood-curdling experiences, or the like; he finds his inspiration in the situation itself. For after all who is the spectator? He is a man, he is Dante himself, and his impressions form a living contrast between what he remembers on earth and what he sees in

Hell. As he enters the forest, the unnatural spectacle confronting him recalls earthly nature to his mind, and the contrast bursts forth:

> Non frondi verdi, ma di color fosco,
>> Non rami schietti, ma nodosi e involti,
>> Non pomi v'eran, ma stecchi con tosco.

> Not green leaves were there, but of a dusky color, not smooth boughs but gnarled and tangled, not fruits but thorns with poison.—*Hell,* xiii, 4–6.

After a few steps human moans strike his ears, but no people are visible; the contrast bursts forth anew, but not in phrases or antitheses: it becomes dramatic and you find it in Dante's every thought and every action. When a person hears a moan, by natural reaction he looks around, because he cannot think of moans without a person moaning. Dante hears and looks, but sees no one! Struck by the weirdness of the situation, he pauses, bewildered:

> Io sentia da ogni parte tragger guai,
>> E non vedea persona che il facesse:
>> Perch'io tutto smarrito m'arrestai.

> I heard wailings uttered on every side, and I saw no one who made them, wherefore, all bewildered, I stopped.— *Hell,* xiii, 22–24.

This is the first impression. The next time, Dante tries to find an explanation for the fact, and he supposes that the wailing comes from people in hiding:

> Io credo ch'ei credette ch'io credesse,
>> Che tante voci uscisser tra quei bronchi
>> Da gente che per noi si nascondesse.

> I believe that he believed that I believed that all these voices issued from amid those trunks from people who because of us had hidden themselves.—*Hell,* xiii, 25–27.

Dante does not accept what is unnatural, his human nature rebels against it, hence the impression on his incredulous imagination will be all the stronger when, at Virgil's request, he breaks a twig off a large thorn-bush:

> E il tronco suo gridò: Perchè mi schiante?
> Da che fatto fu poi di sangue bruno,
> Ricominciò a gridar: Perchè mi scerpi?
> Non hai tu spirto di pietade alcuno?

> And its trunk cried out: "Why dost thou break me?" When
> it had become dark with blood it began again to cry:
> "Why dost thou tear me? hast thou not any spirit of
> pity?"—*Hell,* xiii, 33–36.

Here the fantastic breaks out on every side: not merely moans issue from the trunk, but blood and a voice. Dante is overwhelmed and the marvelous reaches its climax. It has been observed that the idea of this trunk is borrowed from Virgil. But see the difference. In Virgil the contrast is implicit, and is revealed by means of impressions. *Mihi frigidus horror membra quatit. . . . Eloquar, an sileam?* [Fear shrunk my sinews and congealed my blood. . . . Scarce dare I tell the sequel.] [56] in which you see that smoothness of style so typically Virgilian, which makes even horror elegant. Dante needs only a simple exposition, disposing the scene in such a manner that, as it develops naturally, it produces irresistibly an impression of the fantastic. Note here another astonishing example of this: Do you think that Dante pays any attention to the spirit's words? That he feels pity? That he replies? Not at all. The incredible spectacle before his eyes holds him spellbound, leaves him speechless. The spirit speaks and Dante looks on:

> Come d'un stizzo verde, che arso sia
> Dall'un de' capi, che dall'altro geme,
> E cigola per vento che va via;

56. *Aeneid,* ii, 29, 39. Dryden's translation.

Così di quella scheggia usciva insieme
  Parole e sangue: ond'io lasciai la cima
  Cadere, e stetti come l'uom che teme.

As from a green log that is burning at one of its ends, and
  drips from the other, and hisses with the air that is
  escaping, so from that broken twig came out words and
  blood together; whereon I let the tip fall, and stood like
  a man who is afraid.—*Hell,* xiii, 40–45.

What strikes Dante is not the sense of the words, but the fact
that a plant should speak and bleed. That sight affects him so
powerfully that it attracts his vision and excludes all other impressions: all his soul is gathered in his eyes. This is a most perfect example of direct representation. Without the aid of exterior
embellishments, without subjective comments, the Poet contrives to build up gradually the marvel, and the impressions it
creates, to the final climax by merely narrating it, by details
drawn strictly from the situation itself.

What pathos in this fantastic scene! What melancholy in those
leaves of dusky color and in that mysterious moaning which, as
Tasso says,

  . . . un non so che confuso instilla al core
  Di pietà, di spavento, e di dolore!

  . . . instills into one's heart a confused sentiment of pity,
  fright, and grief! [57]

But why, you may ask, are the pathetic details "of dusky
color," "make lament," "wailings uttered," etc., left here in
shadow, the Poet barely sketching them? Because the visual
sense here encroaches on all the other faculties; because wonder
shuts off any other feeling; because if a person is amazed by the
appearance of some new and strange-looking instrument, he will
not even hear the first notes from it. But when the fantastic element is exhausted and the eyes have adjusted themselves to the

57. *Gerusalemme Liberata,* xiii, 4.

scene, then new emotions follow and the pathetic can be developed. You already have a first sample in the words of the spirit. Virgil, too, has his plant speak:

> Quid miserum . . . . laceras? Jam parce sepulto,
> Parce pias scelerare manus . . . .
> Nam Polydorus ego.
> Why dost thou thus my buried body rend?
> O spare the corpse of thy unhappy friend!
> Spare to pollute thy pious hands . . . .
> For I am Polydore.[58]

It is Polydorus speaking to Aeneas. They have fatherland, family, many memories and sorrows in common, and pity is aroused by special circumstances. But in Dante it is a stranger addressing another stranger, and pity springs from a much deeper font. It is a pity exclusively human; the *homo sum,* human nature, wretchedly reversed and debased to the vegetable; it is a human being, who instead of saying, "Why dost thou wound me? Why dost thou pierce me?" is reduced to saying, "Why dost thou break me? Why dost thou tear me?" It is a pity that has its roots in the very heart of the situation, whoever the speaker may be. And the pity becomes heart-rending when the concept breaks out into a vivid antithesis, comparable to Virgil's *qualis erat! quantum mutatus ab illo!* [what it was! how changed from that!],[59]—"we were," and "we are become":

> Uomini fummo, ed or siam fatti sterpi:
>   Ben dovrebb'esser la tua man più pia,
>   Se state fossim'anime di serpi.
> Men we were, and now we are become stocks; truly thy
>   hand ought to be more pitiful had we been souls of
>   serpents.—*Hell,* XIII, 37–39.

58. *Aeneid,* III, 41–42, 45. Dryden's translation.
59. *Ibid.,* II, 274.

It is one stranger speaking to another; yet it is a man speaking to a man.

Between these two impassioned beings, the indignantly moaning spirit and the astounded Dante, rises the serene figure of Virgil. In his calm words you can see the wise man who understands clearly what is incomprehensible to Dante, and who can also understand compassionately the other's sorrow:

> S'egli avesse potuto creder prima,
> Rispose il Savio mio, anima lesa,
> Ciò ch'ha veduto pur con la mia rima,
> Non averebbe in te la man distesa;
> Ma la cosa incredibile mi fece
> Indurlo ad ovra che a me stesso pesa.

> "If he had been able to believe before," replied my Sage, "O injured soul, what he has seen only in my verse, he would not have stretched out his hand on thee; but the incredible thing made me prompt him to an act which weighs on me myself."—*Hell,* xiii, 46–51.

And here the spirit relates his story. Where is Hell now? Where is the tree-trunk? We are in Naples, at the court of King Frederick, in the presence of the Chancellor. If we consider the story, we find in a few lines the essentials of a complete drama: Pier delle Vigne at the zenith of his power and greatness, the war waged against him by envy, the clash that leads to the catastrophe. Pier delle Vigne is merely the narrator; yet if we examine the style, we shall find in him a very fully developed character, a complete poetic personality. We see him in all the vanity of his office, his "glorious office" [*Hell,* xiii, 62], self-satisfied in his power of turning as he chooses the keys of Frederick's heart, jealous of the trust his lord places in him, and intent on removing all others from it. He is a weak man who in his disgrace sees honors turned into mourning, joy into sadness, and who kills himself through "scornful disgust" [*Hell,* xiii, 70], unable to bear his new station; he is a sincere soul who, as he speaks, unwittingly draws his own portrait and reveals himself with utter frankness. What an abundance of significant detail! An entire drama could not reveal him more fully to us: here we have indeed what is called poetic vision, the power to grasp the character in the very act of life! The essence of this character is not greatness or strength, but an exquisite gentleness whose model we have already admired in Francesca da Rimini, and which we remark from his very first words:

> . . . Sì col dolce dir m'adeschi,
> Ch'io non posso tacere; e voi non gravi
> Perch'io un poco a ragionar m'inveschi.

> Thou dost so allure me with sweet speech, that I cannot be silent, and may it not burden you, that I am enticed to talk a little.—*Hell,* xiii, 55–57.

Pier delle Vigne expresses himself not only with delicacy, but also with grace and elegance, as befitting a cultured and intelligent man of exquisite breeding. He employs metaphors, conceits, phrases linked in pairs, such as "morte comune e delle corti vizio," "gl'infiammati infiammar sì Augusto," "i lieti onor tornaro in tristi lutti," "per disdegnoso gusto credendo . . . . fuggir disdegno," "ingiusto fece me contra me giusto" ["common death and vice of the courts," "and they, inflamed, did so inflame Augustus," "my glad honors turned to dismal sorrows," "through scornful disgust thinking to escape scorn," "made me injust toward my just self."—*Hell,* xiii, 66–72]. Why this artificiality? Because Pier delle Vigne is not moved by what he says. If he speaks of his secretarial skill he can come out with that "locking" and "unlocking" of his; if he speaks of his enemies he can well employ a rhetorical personification, the "harlot" who inflames so that the inflamed may inflame Augustus. Not even his suicide moves him. That supreme instant fails to reawaken in him a recollection or an image; it is just a conceit issuing from his lips. One senses in him not the man, but the courtier and the troubadour.

And yet there is one thing, one serious thing alone which

weighs upon him—the infamy his enemies attempt to cast upon his memory, the accusation of treachery. Here lies the pathos of the story; here his imagination warms up, from beneath the courtier's garb emerges the man, and his language becomes simple and eloquent:

> Per le nuove radici d'esto legno
> Vi giuro che giammai non ruppi fede
> Al mio Signor, che fu d'onor sì degno.
> E se di voi alcun nel mondo riede,
> Conforti la memoria mia che giace
> Ancor del colpo che'nvidia le diede.

> By the strange roots of this tree I swear to you, that I never broke faith to my lord who was so worthy of honor. And if one of you returns to the world, let him comfort my memory which yet lies prostrate from the blow that envy gave it.—*Hell,* xiii, 73–78.

To this plant one human thing alone remains alive and present, its memory on earth. It is heart-rending to see a trunk pleading, by its roots still strange, for that part of itself which is still human, its fame: that something alive which is not himself, but rather his old self, for he is now a tree-trunk.

We have now reached the last act, the scene of explanations. Explanation destroys the fantastic; mystery vanishes. When reality was still new and imperfectly known, the human mind lived on fancies, and peopled the earth with fairies, giants, and witches: reality destroyed that world of phantasy. When man was unable to explain natural phenomena, he imagined fantastic creatures that could cause them; science destroyed that world of phantasy, Apollo and his chariot vanished before Galileo's telescope. Here the fantastic element is explained and becomes intelligible: that is to say, it ceases to be fantastic or marvelous and becomes reality—the eternal reality of Hell.

But while fantasticality vanishes pathos remains; indeed it is enhanced, for there is nothing didactical in the explanation. The scientific idea is mentioned incidentally in the line,

Che non è giusto aver ciò ch'uom si toglie.

For it is not just for one to have that of which he deprives
himself.—*Hell,* xiii, 105.

But this idea becomes poetry, because Dante presents it as an
individual case, the soul of a suicide telling its own story from
the time it was separated from the body until Judgment Day.
There is no theorizing, only action, narrated with unusual vigor
and effectiveness of style. The words are rich in meaning and
charged with connotations. In the word "disvelta" [has torn
itself—*Hell,* xiii, 95], one feels not only the separation, but also
the violence of the effort against nature; in "balestra" [flings—
Hell, xiii, 98], not only the fall, but also the impetus and speed
of the fall, and the great distance covered; in the word "finestra"
[window—*Hell,* xiii, 102], one can feel the sighs, laments, and
weeping issuing from that opening.

Why so much feeling and vivacity in the explanation of a fact?
Because we have here a suicide explaining the penalty for suicide
and, by telling the story of any suicide's soul, telling at the same
time the story of his own. Pier delle Vigne has his own self
always present in his imagination: on his lips *a soul,* in his mind
I. So much so that it finally enters the story: the third person
disappears and "parte," "cade," "surge" [departs, falls, rises—
Hell, xiii, 94, 97, 100], are followed by "verremo" and "trascineremo" [we shall go, we shall drag—*Hell,* xiii, 103, 106].

When the explanation is completed the situation appears to be
exhausted, but at this point a new detail comes to rekindle pity:
the remains of the suicide shall hang from the tree, and the soul
shall have it eternally in view, without ever again being able to
vest himself in it. There is an ineffable sadness in Pier delle
Vigne's words:

Qui le trascineremo, e per la mesta
  Selva saranno i nostri corpi appesi,
  Ciascuno al prun dell'ombra sua molesta.

Hither shall we drag them, and through the melancholy
wood shall our bodies be suspended, each on the thorn-
tree of its molested shade.—*Hell,* XIII, 106–8.

His imagination shows him those hanging bodies, "our bodies,"
but that "our" suggests a confused and collective image; he sees
his own body among the others, and feels the need to singularize
that plural:

Ciascuno al prun dell'ombra sua molesta.

Such is this canto, a rich harmony which, starting in a mysterious and fantastic tone, gradually subsides in a sweet melodi-
ous lament.

And now farewell, great characters and great passions! Malebolge awaits us, the seat of the atrocious, the ridiculous, and the
disgusting.

VI

Ugolino

DESCENDING into the Traitors' pit, we find within Dante's Hell a new world of poetry.[60] The place where the Incontinent and the Violent are punished is the realm of great characters and great passions, the realm of tragedy: there we met Francesca, Farinata, Cavalcanti, Pier delle Vigne, Brunetto Latini, Capaneus. In Malebolge [Evil Pouches], where the Frauds are punished, passion becomes vice and force becomes malice; evil or sin no longer originates from an impetuous movement of the soul, but rather from a deep-rooted habit, from an impulse that is almost mechanical, not far from the bestial, so that you can scarcely tell whether man here is man or beast. The hero of that world of low comedy is Vanni Fucci, who says of himself,

> Son Vanni Fucci
> Bestia, e Pistoia mi fu degna tana.

I am Vanni Fucci, beast, and Pistoia was my fitting den.—
Hell, XXIV, 125–26.

Here in the Traitors' pit, at the bottom of Hell, we tumble from man become beast to man become ice, become stone, down

60. First published in *Nuova Antologia* of December, 1869, then in *Nuovi saggi critici* (1873). While based on Lesson VII of the second year's course at Turin,

to a world where motion gradually dies away until life disappears altogether. Hell in this last stage looks to me like a single
evil being, first inflamed and consumed by passions which then
turn into mere mechanical impulses and finally, in his shameful
senility, become in turn impotent desires. It is the story of evil
which at first stirs up all the passions, then in the long run turns
them into habits and vices which finally, wearing out the sinner's
soul, reduce it to torpid infantilism. Humanity in its ideal course
goes from Hell to Paradise, from flesh to spirit; Hell is the world
of the flesh, and its progress is a regression, that is to say a pro-
gressive obfuscation of the spirit until at last it is utterly extinguished. The Traitors' pit marks this final stage and is, properly speaking, the death of the soul, the pure earthly, every trace
of inner life gradually vanishing.

The ancients represented this historical moment by the War of
the Giants, "the Sons of the Earth," against Jove, "the Mind,"
the heavenly nature inferior to them in physical strength and
size, who subdues them with the thunderbolt, product of his
intelligence:

> . . . cui minaccia
> Giove dal cielo ancora, quando tuona.

> Whom Jove still threatens from heaven when he thunders.—
> *Hell*, xxxi, 44–45.

This myth corresponds to the Biblical story of the rebellion of
the angels against God; and here, at the very entrance of the
pit, we find the Giants, and toward the end of it, Lucifer. Mythology and the Bible mingle, two expressions of a single idea.
The Giants are chained; Lucifer is an immense mass of flesh
devoid of intelligence. In them is no life except the material, no
other poetry than that of matter, of giantism, of quantity, of flesh
heaped upon flesh, of flesh as flesh. The Giants are thirty large
spans from the navel up [*Hell*, xxxi, 65]; the face of one is as

---

this essay is the last in point of composition of those in this volume, being
followed only by the study on Dante in the *Storia*.

long and as wide as the huge stone pine-cone that stands at St. Peter's in Rome [*Hell,* xxxi, 58]; Antaeus is compared to the Carisenda [61] [*Hell,* xxxi, 136]; Lucifer is three giants in one, with three heads and six arms, each arm alone many times the size of a giant.[62]

This is the poetry of matter; or rather, strictly speaking, it is not poetry at all, not even the kind inspired by the sublimity of size; for the powerful and sudden impression made by gigantic proportions is enfeebled here, and almost engulfed, by the symbolic details which constantly distract the attention. Allegory dominates: the reader is not absorbed in esthetic contemplation and turns entirely to seek out the meaning of each detail, so that the Giants and Lucifer become symbols of ideas rather than true living realities. Why has Lucifer three faces? Why has each face its own color? What is the meaning of these colors? Why is Antaeus alone left loose among the Giants? And why do the Giants resemble towers? An infinity of "whys" arises, fit prey for the disputations of commentators, the only points of interest in these unesthetic representations. The characters, devoid of spirit, are mere signs of concepts, symbolic figures and nothing else.

Those, then, who like Lamartine or Lamennais censure Dante's Lucifer and find it so much inferior to Milton's Satan, do not realize how absurd it is to compare two such totally different conceptions. Satan is the spirit of evil; he sums up all Hell and has all its passions. Lucifer is the pure earthly; unintelligent and bestial, he is Hell or evil in its final degradation. The former is the rival of God, portrayed in all the fullness of his power and passions, a highly dramatic character; the latter is the vanquished foe of God, crystallized, more like a mechanical motor than a free and conscious agent—an absolutely prosaic character.

61. A leaning tower still standing in Bologna.
62. De Sanctis' misreading: Dante describes Lucifer (*Hell,* xxxiv, 38–42) as having "three faces on his head! one in front . . . the other two . . . above the very middle of each shoulder; and they were joined up to the place of the crest." This implies one head, not three, and two arms, not six. De Sanctis was presumably misled by recalling Lucifer's six wings, six eyes, and three mouths (*Hell,* xxxiv, 46, 53, 57).

Lucifer is the King of Hell only in the sense that he is its basest and most material expression. If by infernal we understand that which is purely material, and therefore prosaic, then neither Charon [*Hell,* III, 118] nor the devils in Malebolge, like Calcabrina or Alichino [*Hell,* XXI, 118], are purely infernal, because spirit continues to speak out in them in some form either comic or tragic. One must go down to Lucifer to find the pure and complete expression of infernality. The waters of Hell mark the same gradation. In the higher regions they are free and flowing, and fall impetuously into Malebolge where they stagnate and putrify. But here, fanned by Lucifer's wings, they freeze, harden, and become a glassy sea, devoid of any trace of life or motion.

The same thing happens to the sinners, in whom every manifestation of life is progressively extinguished. Mummified in that glassy sea, they are all condemned to the same punishment, and that punishment grows in intensity as you proceed from Caina to Antenora and from Tolomea to Giudecca, until it achieves the final obliteration of every sign of life. Cain, Antenor, Ptolemy, Judas are not living persons but mere names. The signs of life and humanity grow progressively weaker, life is gradually petrified. In Caina the damned can still express their sensations: they feel the cold and their teeth chatter "in nota di cicogna" [to the note of the stork—*Hell,* XXXII, 36]; they feel pain and weep. In Antenora they are denied tears: they lie supine, and their first tears turn to glass like "visiere di cristallo" [visors of crystal—*Hell,* XXXIII, 98], filling their eye-sockets and blocking further weeping; but they can still talk. Later they are deprived even of speech, buried completely in the ice through which their bodies show like "festuca in vetro" [straw in glass—*Hell,* XXXIV, 12], with no movement, no weeping, no speech, retaining only the pure and empty material fact of bodily posture.

The only esthetic effects possible here are those which are in fact obtained by the various postures and dispositions of the bodies, now grotesque, now pitiful, always ingenious, clearly carved, thrown into relief by boldly new imagery. We are in the realm of pure description, the poetry of matter. And that this matter is animated, is only feebly intimated here and there, as in the "dattero per figo" [a date for a fig] of Friar Alberigo [*Hell,* xxxiii, 120], or in the grotesque incident of Bocca degli Abati [*Hell,* xxxii, 97]; these are the last flashes of the spirit. The characters are unwilling to talk, and disclose their names only under compulsion; or rather, in a stricter sense we have no real characters but only a list of names, some obscure, some illustrious, but all equally devoid of inner life. What is Cassius? A man "membruto" [large-limbed—*Hell,* xxxiv, 67]. And Brutus is a man who "si storce e non fa motto" [writhes and says not a word —*Hell,* xxxiv, 66].

In this ossified world poetry is wiped out along with life, because at most there can be here only a negative kind of poetry, namely, the impression made on the mind of the spectator Dante by this veritable realm of the dead; it is by this device that the poet has contrived to instill a little lofty and serious poetry into the comic realm of Malebolge, as when he bursts out in his eloquent invective against the popes. But now we come to a device even more ingenious, even richer in poetic effects. Just as the low comedy of Malebolge is converted by poetic art into the sublime indignation of Dante, its spectator, so from this prosaic background rises the desperate grief of Count Ugolino.

But how can Count Ugolino, the most eloquent and modern character in the *Divine Comedy,* find a place here, among these petrified beings?

The fact is that Ugolino is here not as a traitor but as betrayed. To be sure, Count Ugolino, too, is a traitor—that is why he is here. But through a most ingenious device, even as Paolo is bound through eternity to Francesca by love, so is Ugolino bound eternally by hatred to Ruggiero who betrayed him. In Ugolino it is not the traitor who speaks but the one betrayed, the man injured in himself and in his children. To his own crime he makes not the slightest allusion; there is simply no question here of his crime. Fastened to the skull of his foe, an instrument of

eternal justice, he stands there as a living and impassioned witness to the crime of Bishop Ruggiero. A traitor is there, but it
is not Ugolino; it is the head lying under his teeth, motionless,
uttering no cry, every expression of life obliterated from it, the
most perfect model of petrified humanity. Ugolino is the victim
fastened upon that skull by Divine Justice; he is not only the
executioner who carries out orders to which his own spirit remains indifferent: he is also the offended man who adds to these
orders his own hatred and lust for revenge.

The concept of the penalty is the Law of Talion, or the "contrappasso" [retaliation] as Dante would say: Ruggiero becomes
the "fiero pasto" [savage repast] of a man he caused to die of
starvation together with his children. If the concept were left
in these abstract terms, the mode of the punishment would be
disgusting and somewhat grotesque; but here the feeling of disgust is immediately transformed into a sublimity of horror, because the executor of the sentence is not an abstract and indifferent instrument of God, but is the victim himself, sating upon
his enemy his hunger for hatred and revenge. This point has
been overlooked by those commentators who are so tender-
hearted that they hold their noses to shut out the stench of brains
and blood, and protest that the spectacle is indecent and disgusting. Why? Because in the reader there are two impressions
but in the Poet only one. Dante is overwhelmed by the horror
of the situation, he has the image of Ugolino already etched intensely in his imagination and does not linger over the brains
and blood, which enter into his vision as confused elements
barely mentioned as "il teschio e l'altre cose" [the skull and the
other parts—*Hell,* xxxii, 132]. When Ugolino raises his head and
uncovers the skull he has "spoiled," Dante looks at Ugolino, not
at the skull, and then he so horrifies us with the image of the
savage repast, and of Ugolino wiping his mouth on the hair of
that head used as a napkin, that our imagination is held spellbound, incapable of turning its attention to the rest of the
spectacle.

If one wishes to appreciate a work of poetry, he must relive in his mind that first creative moment of the poet. Unfortunately, we memorize this canto of Count Ugolino when we are very young, and call it beautiful on our teacher's word; when our own esthetic sense awakens, it is already too late: our first spontaneous impression is irreparably lost, we cannot recapture or rejuvenate it. Having lost that first warmth of response, we no longer feel but analyze; we fail to grasp the conception as a whole, and the less we understand the whole, the more we linger on details, so that quite naturally we discover brains and blood and hold our noses. But if one has the power to wipe out those later impressions and to renew his esthetic sense, he will not see here tendons, nerves, and brains—Dante's imagination is swift and leaves him no time for that—but will stand terrified and as if annihilated before that colossal apparition full of hatred (not a sectarian hatred,[63] but the human hatred of an offended father), and will surmise some frightful story that could have led a human being to so beastly a deed.

When a character of such ideal magnitude holds the stage, he draws the eyes and mind of the spectator to the exclusion of any other sight or impression. And notice what grandeur of proportions Dante has given to this Ugolino! You would expect to find that this gesture of such extraordinary ferocity would be an adequate expression of his hate, and suffice indeed to strike our imagination with terror; but no! Ugolino is more savage than his deed, he is revealed by that gesture but not appeased by it, like an unsatisfied artist who cannot find his ideal expressed in his work, and despairs of ever achieving it. Ugolino's grief is "desperate," not sated, not placated by that vengeance; his grief is still so alive and powerful that only in thinking of it "pur pensando" [*Hell,* xxxiii, 6], he weeps as if he had just now been hurt. In Shakespeare too we see a father whose children have been murdered. A friend cries to him, "What, man! ne'er pull

---

63. Aroux says, "All the hate of the sectarian, incarnated in a father crazed with vengeance." I do find the father here, but I do not see the sectarian. (Author's note)

your hat upon your brows . . . . Let's make us med'cines of our great revenge,/To cure this deadly grief." "He has no children," answers MacDuff.[64] A terrifying answer intimating the hopelessness of vengeance in a father who cannot kill the children of the man who killed his. But Dante's concept is even higher: Ugolino, holding his enemy under his teeth, remains unsatisfied, and not because he desires a fiercer vengeance but because no vengeance can ever assuage his grief or equal his hatred. His grief is infinite; even more passionately wild than his deed is his soul.

A certain resemblance has been noted between the first words of Ugolino and those of Francesca;[65] the same words set to different music, as there is in the two situations at once a point of similarity and one of difference, a similarity of concept with diversity of emotion. Both Francesca and Ugolino recollect the past with grief; they both yield to Dante's request, and weep and speak at the same time. But for Francesca it is a voluptuous and happy past that is now one with her present misery, and her enamored soul renders her weeping gentle and her sorrow beautiful; hence the softness and suavity of such lines as

> Nessun maggior dolore
> Che ricordarsi del tempo felice
> Nella miseria . . . .
> Ma se a conoscer la prima radice
> Del nostro amor tu hai cotanto affetto,
> Farò come colui che piange e dice.

> There is no greater woe than the remembering in misery the happy time . . . . But if thou hast so great desire to know the first root of our love, I will do like one who weeps and tells.—*Hell*, v, 121-26.

For Ugolino past and present are of the same hue, are a single grief arousing savage emotion and whipping up rage; you can see, glaring through his tears, the gloomy flame of hatred. His

64. *Macbeth*, Act IV, Scene 3.
65. Thou shalt see me speak and weep together (*Hell*, xxxiii, 9). I will do like one who weeps and tells (*Hell*, v, 26). (Author's note)

"gnawing" is represented together with his weeping; this man weeps, but his weeping frightens you; you feel that at any moment, in the midst of his tears, his grief may turn to rage and he may fall again to biting that skull. He speaks and weeps, not in compliance with Dante's request, like gentle Francesca, but in hatred, so that his words may bear fruit of infamy, "fruttino infamia," for the traitor. Dante's final brush stroke is the terrible phrase "tal vicino" [such a neighbor]. "Neighbor" suggests a benign idea of friendship and familiarity among men living and dealing with one another, but on Ugolino's lips it is a bitter irony.

Through this pathetic conception poetry enters even into this prosaic lowest depth of Hell, thawing its ice and imbuing it with life. And this poetry is none other than the portrayal of Treachery, the crime punished here in all its gradations; a portrayal not made by the traitor, whose frozen heart is hardened and dead to every feeling, as motionless as that skull of his, but rather by the victim turned executioner.

With the creation of this situation the frozen prosaic realm of necessity becomes again the free realm of art. Ugolino as a traitor is among the frozen spirits; as a victim, placed there by Divine Judgment, with his head like a "hat" on the wrongdoer's head, he is not only a fatal instrument of eternal law, but also the wronged person bringing to the execution of his task all his passions as man and as father. In the representation of the punishment the concept of justice is therefore taken for granted; the Poet makes no allusion to it, Ugolino is unaware of it. Bertrand de Born is merely a sinner and a damned soul; he recognizes the justice of his punishment and can say,

Così s'osserva in me il contrappasso.

Thus the retribution is observed in me.—*Hell,* xxviii, 142.

In his case the poetical interest can rise only from our horror and amazement at so unusual a penalty—a bust holding its truncated head by the hair, "pesol con mano" [dangling it in hand—*Hell,*

XXVIII, 122]; horror and amazement that turn to intellectual satisfaction as the penalty is explained and legitimized. But Ugolino here is not the sinner, the damned soul, not even the executor of Divine Justice except quite unconsciously; one thing alone he knows: that he has his enemy's skull under his teeth and is venting upon it his hatred. Dante himself is struck only by the personal element in that act, by the outpouring of hatred from an offended man:

> O tu che mostri per sì bestial segno
> Odio sopra colui che tu ti mangi,
> Dimmi il perchè, diss'io, per tal convegno:
> Ché, se tu a ragion di lui ti piangi . . . . , etc.

> "O thou that by so bestial a sign showest hatred against him
> whom thou art eating, tell me the wherefore," said I,
> "with this compact, that if thou with reason complainest
> of him . . . ."—*Hell,* XXXII, 133–36.

Thus Ugolino is a complete poetical character who can reveal all the richness of his inner life.

With a few quick strokes the Poet has hewn this colossal statue of hatred, a hatred more violent than that "bestial sign," which has already made such a deep impression on his mind. But within that hatred grows love and the murky gloom of that soul is gradually dissolved into the most tender feelings. This man hates violently because he has loved intensely. His hatred is infinite because infinite was his love, and his grief is desperate because no vengeance can equal the injury he has suffered. All this you find mingled and fused in his story, and you cannot tell whether, in that story, horror dominates or rather pity. A curse mingles with his tears, and in the same phrase there are often hatred and love, rage and tenderness together. The last sound of Ugolino's words as he calls upon his children is lost in the crackling of the hated bones under his teeth.

The background of the story is summarized in a few very swift strokes which bring before us his life as a prisoner, when months and years, which fly like hours to the man absorbed in business, seem centuries counted minute by minute. Ugolino is locked in a prison, whose scant light comes through a tiny hole on which he keeps his eyes fastened; his timepiece is the moon, by which he keeps count of the months of his detention. That narrow jail compared to a "mew," that small "slit," and those hours counted one by one, are the whole story of the prisoner in its visible form. His state of mind is depicted with equally firm strokes. Two thoughts nourish the solitary soul of Ugolino: the uncertainty of his fate and the persistent malice of his enemies. What torments the prisoner most is uncertainty, as he constantly wonders, "What will become of me?" His imagination, exasperated by suffering and solitude, yields to alternating hopes and fears. Ignorant of his fate, he hopes and fears and cannot drive from his mind the thought of death. And he remains in that state until "the evil dream" comes that "rends . . . the veil of the future."

Of all this intimate story the Poet describes only the last phase, but this suffices for even a reader of mediocre imagination to divine the rest. The description is given in that suggestively musical manner which is the greatest charm of poetry. The "mal sonno!" [evil dream]. That "mal," imprecation and curse upon the dream, gives a glimpse of so many hopes destroyed, so many illusions dispelled! The dream is a veil through which the anxiety of the waking hours is easily perceived: reality is revealed underneath the fancy. Ruggiero, Gualandi, Sismondi, Lanfranchi, so cruel to him and his children, are always present in the prisoner's mind, and now appear to him in the dream as hunting a wolf and its whelps. His eyes see animals, but his mind feels confusedly that these animals are really himself and his children, and the wolf and whelps become transformed, with human designations, into "father and sons." If a man dreams of being pursued and tries to flee, though he lies motionless in bed he feels his legs tired and aching. That poor wolf is really "the father," Ugolino himself; he cannot run and already feels in his sides "the sharp fangs":

In picciol corso mi pareano stanchi
  Lo padre e i figli, e con le acute zane
  Mi parea lor veder fender li fianchi.

After short course, the father and his sons seemed to me
  weary, and it seemed to me that I saw their flanks
  ripped by the sharp fangs.—*Hell,* xxxiii, 34–36.

Here new actors come on the stage. Ugolino is not alone; his
children appear just at the moment of crisis and make his grief
more poignant. They too have dreamed; they are hungry and ask
for bread. Ugolino compares his own dream to his children's, and
comes to his final conclusions: death, and death by starvation!
That was the "foreboding" in his heart. It all seems so clear to
him that he cannot understand how Dante can fail to sense it and
be as moved as he was himself:

Ben se' crudel, se tu già non ti duoli,
  Pensando ciò ch'al mio cor s'annunziava;
  E se non piangi, di che pianger suoli?

Truly thou art cruel if already thou dost not grieve, at
  thought of that which my heart was foreboding: and if
  thou dost not weep, at what art thou wont to weep?—
  Hell, xxxiii, 40–42.

When shaken with suffering, we wish that all would share our
affliction and are pained by the indifference of others. Among the
populace, a mother who fears that her son may have been killed
goes running through the streets beside herself, asking the
passers-by, "Have you seen him?" as if all should know what
she means and what grieves her. In his own and in his children's
dream Ugolino already sees his whole story; when he raises his
eyes toward Dante, he sees a face rather curious than sympathetic,
not reflecting his own emotion; he is irritated, he almost feels that
the man has no human soul, and inveighs against him with
sudden blunt reproof. His harsh words, springing from the
sincerity of an impatient and angry grief, do not provoke

Dante's wrath but, on the contrary, increase his sympathy and almost draw premature tears to his eyes.

This presentation may appear meager to those who are inclined to rhetoric and analysis, to those accustomed to reduce sentiments to pills, to thin out *The last hours of a condemned man* [66] into a whole volume. This is a masterpiece in the Dantesque manner, which is the grand manner, painting with broad quick strokes, leaving large patches of shadow illumined by vivid flashes of light. Everything is concrete; everything is narrated rather than described or merely represented, but narrated in such a way that our imagination, stirred to swift activity, fills the gaps and divines the inner story. It is rather a sketch than a painting, but a sketch that leads the reader to make at once his own painting. This is possible because the painting already exists in the Poet's mind; existing there, it is revealed so clearly in the sketch that the poet would be annoyed, like Ugolino, if the reader were to remain cold and appear not to understand. The greatness of genius consists not in what it can say but in what it makes you divine.

In what follows, the whole significance derives from the presence of the children. If Ugolino were alone his story would end here, for he is too proud a man to linger on the details of his agony. But the offense he suffered was not his own death, it was that of his children. This makes him an exceedingly interesting character. You notice it in the soft and affectionate tone of his speech when he first introduces the children:

> Pianger sentii fra 'l sonno i miei figliuoli,
> Ch'eran con meco, e dimandar del pane.

> I heard my sons, who were with me, wailing in their sleep,
> and asking for bread.—*Hell,* xxxiii, 38–39.

It is this sight which moves him so deeply as to provoke his disdainful and blunt apostrophe to Dante, not sufficiently moved at the thought of what was "foreboding" to Ugolino's paternal

66. An obvious reference to Victor Hugo's novel *Le dernier jour d'un condamné* (1829).

heart. That which his heart was foreboding was not his own death, but the sight of his children's death; when he heard "the door below of the horrible tower being nailed up," his first reaction was to look at his children, who had heard nothing and were unaware of their fate. A vein of tenderness penetrates his savage nature; his paternal love adds a certain beauty to his character, softens his tone. The rough, harsh music with which he began and with which he will end, that music of bestial hatred, here takes on a tender-sweet suavity almost elegiac.

We have here a new Ugolino who cannot be envisaged in isolation, and we must study him in his children to understand his infinite grief.

His children are young, innocent of the passions and warfare of politics, new to the vicissitudes of life; they are here without knowing why; their father is their whole world. The ideal of this "età novella" [young age] is a kind of serene vitality. In the soul of a child there is always something that smiles, an inner joy that shines through in the purity and softness of his features. His presence soothes the tensions of the human tragedy; it smooths the wrinkles on Goetz's face when, home from the wars, he plays with his child; it makes Andromache laugh amid her tears—"she laughed weeping," Homer says, when she saw her child fondled by his father.[67] This is the pure ideal of the child, Homer's serene ideal. The child is quite devoid of self-consciousness, of that formidable "tomorrow" that devours us, and we, swept along in the storm of life, take pleasure at times in contemplating his peace. But what if that storm should threaten to engulf his poor innocent head? Nothing can equal the pathos of a situation such as this. The less the child is aware of the danger, the greater is our torment. We put ourselves in his place; we become his own consciousness and tremble at the thought of the dangers hanging over him, dangers of which he remains ignorant by a sort of unconscious irony.

I once saw a child play with the pall of the coffin where his father was shortly to be laid, and a man wipe his eyes and say,

67. Goethe, *Goetz von Berlichingen*, I, 3; *Iliad*, VI, 471, 484.

"Poor child!" That man was an indifferent spectator; what if the spectator had been the father, a father who knew he was to die together with his children, while the children were ignorant of their fate? That is the situation of Count Ugolino. You have here a difference, a contrast of attitudes and emotions, the very dualism from which drama is born. You already can see it vigorously depicted, with immense compassion, at the very beginning of the scene. Ugolino, on hearing the door of the tower being locked, looks at his children's faces. He wants to say, "Poor children!" but he dare not; only his eyes utter it. His crushing grief deprives him of speech and of tears. His whole life is summoned to that glance:

>   . . . guardai
> Nel viso a' miei figliuoli senza far motto.
> I' non piangeva, sì dentro impietrai.

> I looked on the faces of my sons without saying a word. I
>   did not weep, I was so turned to stone within.—*Hell,*
>   XXXIII, 47–49.

But the children weep. Not because they understand, but because they see their father looking at them with such an expression:

> Piangevan elli; ed Anselmuccio mio
> Disse: Tu guardi sì, padre, che hai?

> They were weeping; and my poor little Anselm said, "Thou
>   lookest so, father, what ails thee?"—*Hell,* XXXIII, 50–51.

"Thou lookest so." Little Anselm is incapable of defining or explaining that look. That "so" means "in such an unnatural and extraordinary manner." "What ails thee?" asks the child. The anguish is all in the meaning of that speechless look, and in the innocence of that query "What ails thee?" with its accompanying tears. The contrast comes forth naturally and for all its depth is so crystal-clear that it takes you immediately into the heart of the situation. If a painter were to select a grouping to present in a synthesis the essential traits of this tragedy, the grouping should be this one, for we have here the really decisive moment of the story, and we discern already in the attitude of the father and the children all the motives of the highest kind of pathos.

The first thought of the father is his children, and the first thought of the children is their father. "What ails thee?" they ask. If the father did not speak or weep before, it was because he was "petrified," but now it is in order not to grieve his children more; since he loves them he must conceal his feelings. In our afflictions we must have an outlet; we could not bear our sorrows unless, urged by a beneficent natural impulse, we could shout, curse, weep, tear our hair, or bite our hands. Yet this father must swallow his grief in silence, repress every natural impulse, control his expression and his gestures, must become a statue instead of a man—the statue of desperation:

Però non lacrimai, nè rispos'io
   Tutto quel giorno, nè la notte appresso.

I shed no tear for that; nor did I answer all that day, nor the night after.—*Hell,* xxxiii, 52–53.

The repression is all the more violent because of the great tenderness of feeling revealed in such phrases as "What ails thee?" and "my little Anselm," which recall, in a situation now so altered, so many dear family joys now past. But this long repression of feelings that keep straining a whole day and night for utterance, this tragedy that takes place solely and entirely within, lacking outward expression, is the negation of all poetry because it is carried beyond form and hence beyond its life. Esthetically, only that which can be represented has life. Even as the frozen soul of the traitor marks the end of Infernal life, so the impassivity of Ugolino marks the death of emotion, being without tears, without speech, without gesture, without expression.

This silent shutting up of the soul within its own despair can be sublime at times, provided it finds its own expression, as it did for that artist who rendered the ineffable grief of Agamemnon before Iphigenia's sacrifice, by covering his face with a veil.[68] But even in such a case, the story must end quickly, death must come at once to terminate a situation which would become prosaic or ridiculous if prolonged. Beautiful is Caesar as he wraps himself in his toga—provided that he dies soon after.

Dante, however, did something even better: he changed the statue back into a man. If a poet expects me to be interested in his characters, he must never let the human visage, the *homo sum,* be obliterated in them, no matter how extraordinary be the situations in which he places them; their humanity, on the contrary, must always be apparent, so that I can better perceive their struggle and feel the endlessness of their mute despair. During that night of silence, hunger had wasted and transformed the faces of father and sons. When daylight filtered in, the appearance of the children struck Ugolino suddenly, bringing upon him a natural moment of forgetfulness in which he gives vent to his feelings; he bursts out with a gesture of rage all the more savage and bestial because of the violence of the preceding repression and the suddenness of his impression on beholding so unexpectedly vivid a sight.

> Come un poco di raggio si fu messo
> Nel doloroso carcere, ed io scorsi
> Per quattro visi il mio aspetto stesso,
> Ambo le mani per dolor mi morsi.

> When a little ray made its way into the woeful prison, and I
> discerned by their four faces my own very aspect, I bit
> both my hands for woe.—*Hell,* xxxiii, 55-58.

This man who in a momentary fit of fury bites both hands, is already in anticipation the one who is fixed and eternized in Hell, with his teeth, "come d'un can, forti" [strong as a dog's], upon

---

68. The Greek painter Timanthes so represented the sacrifice of Iphigenia. A presumed copy of this painting was found in Pompeii, and can now be seen among the *Affreschi Pompeiani* in the National Museum of Naples, where De Sanctis may well have seen it. He refers to this painting also in his essay on Farinata.

the skull of his enemy. But how deep the woe that aroused such fury! "Per quattro visi!" [By their four faces!] You find here fused together all that is most tender and most savage; so fused together that while in the expression you must have a "first" and a "later," in your imagination you see it as a single act, a single moment of emotion complex and nameless. You cannot imagine that father biting his hands without seeing him at the same time gazing into those four faces.

The impression this gesture makes on the children enhances its effect and carries it to an irresistible quickening of our innermost feelings. Earlier, when the door was locked, they did not understand that first fixed and twisted look on their father's face. "Tu guardi sì, padre, che hai?" [Thou lookest so, father, what ails thee?] Now they not only fail to understand the biting of his hands, they misconstrue it entirely, "pensando ch'io il fessi per voglia/Di manicar" [thinking I did it through desire of eating—*Hell*, xxxiii, 59–60]. With childish unawareness of his passions they give that gesture its immediate literal meaning. They feel hungry and judge by their own feelings: to bite for them means to eat. Their father eating his own hands from hunger is such a horrible thing, stirs in them such fright, that an intelligent actor, by that alone, should be able to grasp all that is implied in the cry, "Father!" and in the sudden rising of the four children, lying on the floor exhausted by starvation. That cry as they rise up has the power to stop the father, to restore his mastery over himself, to shock him back from that moment of oblivion, to make him remember that as a father he cannot permit himself any human weakness. Their offer of themselves as repast to their father is not really a sublime sacrifice of filial devotion—a sentiment too virile for tender breasts—but rather an offer transformed immediately into a prayer for something they desire and invoke, for the end of their misery: "Kill us! stop our agony!"

> . . . tu ne vestisti
> Queste misere carni, e tu le spoglia.

> . . . thou didst clothe us with this wretched flesh, and do
> thou strip it off.—*Hell*, xxxiii, 62–63.

"Wretched flesh!" They already feel their lives dissolve and
fail. "Wretched" here means exhausted, already penetrated by
death. Those who explain this word in a spiritual sense, fishing
for some theological concept, would make worthy companions
for Father Cesari, who, among his numerous Dantean "beauties,"
finds here something ugly, a fact beyond the natural and the
possible—just at this point, in the chorus of these four immortal
children which has been the admiration of the centuries!

Ugolino turned father is turned again to stone:

> Quietaimi allor, per non farli più tristi;
> Quel dì e l'altro stemmo tutti muti.
>
> I quieted me then, not to make them more sad: that day
> and the next we all stayed dumb.—*Hell*, xxxiii, 64–65.

Those "u's" of the second line make you shiver, so gloomy is
their sound. It is a silence of repression for the father, of agony
for the children, but it is not a prosaic matter of "I answered not
and shed no tears"; it is a silence charged with meaning and
with eloquence by Ugolino's cry announcing the approach of the
end. It is not just the body which is prostrated by hunger now—
the soul too is stricken and can stand no more; Ugolino calls
upon the earth to open up and swallow him, curses it, and calls
it cruel:

> Ahi cruda terra, perchè non ti apristi?
>
> Ah, thou hard earth! why didst thou not open?—*Hell*,
> xxxiii, 66.

It is an impatient cry for death. The strength to suffer has
failed, worn out by that long repression, by that long effort
against nature. But the relentless poet will give Ugolino no truce
until the dagger has once more been thrust deep into his heart by
the hand of those terrible children, innocently unaware of the
wounds they are inflicting:

Gaddo mi si gittò disteso a' piedi,
  Dicendo: Padre mio, chè non m'aiuti?
Gaddo threw himself stretched out at my feet, saying: "My
  father, why dost thou not help me?"—*Hell,* xxxiii, 68–69.

as if his father could, and did not want to aid him.

Then comes the catastrophe. The father sees them die, as truly
as Dante sees him; he sees them die one by one, and it was for
him a torture of three days:

Quivi morì; e come tu mi vedi,
  Vid'io cascar li tre ad uno ad uno
  Fra il quinto dì e il sesto. . . .
Here he died: and, even as thou seest me, I saw the three fall
  one by one between the fifth day and the sixth. . . .—
  Hell, xxxiii, 70–72.

There is no empty detail here. That spectacle of death is repeated four times, at long intervals, within the space of three
days, and a father had to see that while remaining quiet, keeping
the torture to himself, repressing within himself nature and
humanity!

Then comes the outburst. His feelings, long repressed, break
out. But this is not the release of a pent-up human emotion,
eloquent, conscious, active, intelligible to himself and to others;
it is the explosion of a broken spirit, more like convulsions or
delirium than speech. These are not thoughts, scarcely even words
that he utters, but cries, interjections; expression in its elementary
state, affection in its instinctive and animal form. While his
children were alive he dared not call them by name, he could
not express his tenderness or his grief. Behold him now groping
over each one and calling them, calling them for three days: [69]

---

69. This appears to be another numerical lapsus as the text is usually read,
"E due dì. . . ." (And for two days. . . .) The source of the error can be seen
in the "three days" quoted a few lines above. We have changed the Norton
translation from "two" to "three" to conform to De Sanctis' version.

E tre dì li chiamai poi che fur morti.

And for three days I called them after they were dead.—*Hell,*
XXXIII, 74.

Before his body died the man in him was dead. What had
survived was the beast, torn between love and fury, a beast whose
frightful roars expressed pity or rage, we wonder which. There
is here no longer any analysis, or thought, or a single sentiment,
clear and distinct. The act of calling his children was sorrow,
tenderness, rage; it was all of Ugolino changed into an instinct
and expressed by a roar. This man already feral is surrounded
by a halo of darkness, like the final silence and the final agony
in a death chamber. Such is the dreadful effect of those last
obscure moments.

Poscia più che il dolor potè il digiuno.

Then fasting was more powerful than woe.—*Hell,* XXXIII, 75.

This line is crystal-clear in its literal sense, and obviously
means: what sorrow could not do, hunger achieved; sorrow could
not kill him, starvation killed him. Yet it is a line thick with ob-
scurity and hidden meanings, because of the swarm of sentiments
and images it arouses, because of the many "perchances" it
suggests, all intensely poetical. Perhaps he called on death,
bewailing that grief could not kill him and that he must wait
for the slow death by starvation: this would be a sentiment of
desperation. Perhaps he did not cease calling his children until
hunger, more powerful than sorrow, deprived him of the
strength to do so, first his sight failing him and then his voice:
this would be a sentiment of tenderness. Perhaps while nature
drove his teeth into the "wretched flesh," that flesh became the
flesh of his enemy in his imagination, in a last delirium of hunger
and vindictiveness, a delirium that Dante realized in Hell by
perpetuating that last gesture and that last thought: this would
be a sentiment of canine fury.

All this is possible; all this can be conceived, thought, imagined; each conjecture finds its basis in some word, in the possible interpretation of some idea. The reader's imagination is struck, energized, driven to activity; it is not set on any definite reality and wanders over those last hours of human degradation. Standing out clearly above these vague and perplexed impressions, those four innocents are seen stretched on the ground, their names repeated for three days by a voice, one knows not whether human or bestial. But the echo of those names lingers in the mind of the reader, who finds his own feeling expressed in the last words of Dante. While the wild beast twists its eyes and fastens its teeth again in the skull, the reader sees those four poor youths, and calls them by name, one by one, and exclaims, "They were innocent!"

> Innocenti facea l'età novella
>   . . . Uguccione e il Brigata,
> E gli altri duo che il canto suso appella.

> Their young age . . . made Uguccione and Il Brigata innocent, and the other two that my song names above.— *Hell,* XXXIII, 88–90.

The weeping of Ugolino is fury; Dante's pity takes the form of indignation, of imprecation, and in his wrath the Poet evokes a strange manner of destruction for this city that doomed to death four innocents:

> Muovansi la Capraia e la Gorgona,
> E faccian siepe ad Arno in su la foce,
> Sì ch'egli annieghi in te ogni persona.

> Let Caprara and Gorgona move and make a hedge for Arno at its mouth, so that it may drown every person in thee. —*Hell,* XXXIII, 82–84.

I know not who is the more ferocious, Ugolino with his teeth fastened to the skull of his traitor, or Dante, who in order to avenge four innocents would doom to death the innocents of an entire city, fathers, children, and children's children: Biblical wrath, a savage passion in savage times, such as could make possible a conception of Hell essentially poetic, but underneath which lies a whole world of history.

Everything here is in a terrible harmony, the poet, the actor, the spectator. Like sinner like narrator, like spectator like poet; they complement and explain each other. Everything is portrayed larger than life. You do not find yet the true human dimensions, the life-sized statue, but the Pyramid, the Colossus, the gigantic, with which primitive antiquity first gave confused expression to conscious emotion, to the feeling for greatness, for the infinite, which was all the more awe-inspiring as it was less clearly analyzed. This is the secret of these powerful Dantean sketches, so scantily developed, so full of shadows and gaps; by the simplicity of their outline and by effective chiaroscuro, they magnify dimensions and sentiments. Often it is a single image that works the miracle, snatching you from the realm of reality and lifting you beyond the laws of plausibility into the realm of immensity. Of this sort is the wiping of Ugolino's mouth on the hair of the spoiled skull, and the *moving* of Capraia and Gorgona. That wiping of the mouth appalls you, not by the gesture in itself, but because it presents you the whole face of Ugolino with features idealized to befit that gesture; it puts before you the preternatural expression of immense hate, and by that you conceive the infinite.

The poet says,

> . . . io vidi duo ghiacciati in una buca
> Sì che l'un capo all'altro era cappello.
> E come il pan per fame si manduca,
> Così il sopran li denti all'altro pose
> Là 've 'l cervel s'aggiunge con la nuca.

> I saw two frozen in one hole, so that the head of one was a hood for the other. And as bread is devoured for hunger, so the upper one set his teeth upon the other where the brain joins with the nape.—*Hell,* xxxii, 125–29.

You have here the most precise details, given in clear and simple terms; and yet you find all this prosaic because you see nothing beyond its literal sense. The outline is clear-cut, the vision is evident, but it suggests nothing besides what it shows, and the reader's imagination remains inert. Poetry begins, as the solemn and epic intonation of the line proclaims, when

La bocca sollevò dal fiero pasto
  Quel peccator . . . .
From his savage repast that sinner raised his mouth . . . .
  —*Hell,* xxxiii, 1–2.

even before he speaks, with a single unexpected and appalling gesture—though a most natural one to him—Ugolino stands before you complete, body and soul.

A similar effect is produced likewise by the line

Muovansi la Capraia e la Gorgona,
  Let Caprara and Gorgona move.—*Hell,* xxxiii, 82.

where Nature itself is called upon to break its laws, abandon its immobility, acquire consciousness, life, and motion, and rush to punish the guilty city. A catastrophe so extraordinary in nature, a penalty so far out of the normal run of things, raises the crime to its own level and gives it colossal proportions; a profile out of Aeschylus, the primitive and integrally epic style, not yet invaded by lyrical or dramatic elements; an enormous block of granite that drives you back in wonder and awe, of which the chisel dare not seek out the veins and bare the inner structure.

But Dante does dare to wield the chisel, and to draw lines, to carve figures that recall the most profound dramatic situations, and achieve the highest lyrical effects. Within the bare and severe greatness of a gigantic and unchanging nature, there emerge a variety of conflicting elements, shaping into a real-life scene presented in its most tenderly human aspects. On his Infernal pedestal, Ugolino first appears with his face smitten by Eternity, his features rigid, a statue of hatred, of a hatred eternal, unsated, immense with an Alpine immensity, inaccessible to our imagination. But lo, Ugolino comes to life, tears tremble on his lids, his hands accompany with their gestures his words, and the most varied emotions appear on his expressive face. He is a man again, a father among his children. The finest gradations of a dramatic situation profoundly intuited are visible here, in a *crescendo* that takes you from pathos to grief, from grief to despair, down to the death of the soul, to human degradation, to that being who with twisted eyes sets his teeth once more into the skull and is crystallized again into an eternity of hatred. And all these gradations spring forth from the children's lips. They are the real tormentors of their father; their every word is a stab, but they remain unaware of it, they love him dearly. Their innocence, their love become instruments of torture for their father and crush his soul, turning him into the wild beast that stands there on his Infernal pedestal. His paternal tenderness and pity become savagery and rage, his weeping turns to biting, to the infinite terror and horror of the spectators. Dante too is overcome by the same violent feelings. He too turns savage; you almost feel that if he could lay hands on those Pisans, "vituperio delle genti" [reproach of the people—*Hell,* xxxiii, 79], he would turn on them and bite them.

To throw figures and situations so tender, gentle, lovable, into the midst of conceptions so savage; to preserve unity of concept, design, coloring amid such a great variety of gradations; to strike many chords without forgetting the principal *motif,* and indeed to make use of that very diversity to lead us back to the same *motif;* to imagine the newest, the most unexpected, the most piteous situations while filling them with darkness, silence, despair, and monotony; to introduce contrasts so real, so natural, so intimate into such a great unity; to develop images and sentiments to some grandiose, or savage, or sublime climax, achieving this with such a fusion of colors, such fine shadings, such spontaneity and openness of human nature that nothing seems artificial or exaggerated but, on the contrary, everything seems true, natural, clear, and inevitable, and we are deeply touched in our human nature—these are the miracles of art!

Precisely because this is the most finely shaded and developed of all the Dantean sketches, it is also the most popular and modern. Francesca and Ugolino are the two episodes that have remained alive in all the civilized world, even among the uncultured classes. The excessively concentrated, fixed, rough-hewn quality which somehow seems characteristic of all the Dantean conceptions, is here dissolved, revealing contrasts and gradations that unveil to your view the great depths of the human heart.

But even as Francesca has remained unique in the field of Italian poetry, so the sentiment from which Dante here has drawn such varied dramatic effects can be said to be foreign to our Muse. We never meet again that father and those children. Family sentiment is a plant almost exotic on our soil; neither in prose nor in rhyme are we shown by our poets the sentiments of a sister, a wife, a mother, a father, or a son. It cannot be said that these sentiments are alien to our people; on the contrary, they have deep roots, especially among the common people. But as our poets, surrounded by natural beauty, lack a sincere and intimate sentiment for nature, even so, surrounded by examples of family affection, they lack a feeling for the intimacies of domestic life amid which the Muse of the North dwells so often and with such natural ease. We like fantastic and extraordinary situations, superficial loves, quick and vivid impressions, unexpected and spectacular scenes, a life of pomp and state. Friendship, family, the cult of nature, a simple and modest life comforted by domestic affection, are subjects inadequate to rouse our mobile imagination. We admire Antigone, Merope, Laocoön, Andromache, but with an admiration which is artistic and therefore superficial. We do not see ourselves in them, not our whole selves. These affections so pure, so simple, vanish for us with our earliest years, and we never find them again in the tumult of the world. Could Alfieri represent Merope? [70]

Dante found his successors outside of Italy.

70. Title of another tragedy by Alfieri, which De Sanctis found inadequate in its representation of domestic affections.

VII

The Divine Comedy: *Translation by F. Lamennais with an Introduction on Dante's Life, Ideas, and Works*

HERE is a new work on Dante.[71] It is Lamennais' testament, interrupted by his death.

I used to think that a French translation of Dante was, rather than a difficult undertaking, a hopeless one, but Lamennais has achieved a miracle: he has forced the French language to obey Dante. His version is literal. In this type of translation the letter usually kills the spirit; if at best it gives you the meaning, it seldom reproduces the poetry of the original. But under the pen of Lamennais the bare letter becomes thought and image, coloring and music. His substitution of word for word is done with such keen understanding of the text, with such scrupulous exactness, that the thought passes clearly from one language into the other.[72]

71. First published in *Il Cimento* (Torino, series III, anno iii, luglio 1855), pp. 3–15, then in *Saggi critici* (1866). In date of publication it is the earliest of the essays in this volume, though composed at a date slightly later than that of the original text of *Pier delle Vigne,* q.v. The work reviewed appeared in 1855 as part of the series of Lamennais' *Oeuvres posthumes* (ed. Forgues; Paulin et Le Chevalier, Paris, 1855–58, 5 vols.).

72. Except in a few cases such as "We see . . . things that are distant, as well as the supreme Ruler illumes them." The translator did not correctly understand the line, "cotanto ancor ne splende il sommo Duce" [So much the su-

This is already an achievement, considering how difficult it is to understand Dante, even for an Italian; but it is the least of Lamennais' achievements. He discerns not just the Italian word for which he seeks adequate translation, but Dante's thought, alive and entire, which becomes French with all its accessories, its coloring and its harmony. He achieves this with such clarity and ease, without effort, without trite phrases, that the thought seems born in French.

It is a marvelous thing to see that such an exceptionally vigorous translation can at the same time be strictly literal. With a skillful placing of words, with bold inversions, he creates a sort of rhythmic prose that imitates the Dantean harmony; by the use of bold ellipses, asyndeta, brachylogies, and a masterful use of particles, he preserves all the energy and brevity of the Dantesque manner.[73] Dante expresses profound thoughts with vivid images and often with simplicity; even metaphysics becomes concrete under his pen. Lamennais often rises to this plastic perfection by the judicious use of poetic license. With great skill he borrows from the early French classics, so that his coloring and constructions have a flavor of antiquity that recalls Amyot and Montaigne.

Without detaining you longer with general remarks, let me compare this version with another, also literal, by Brizeux, taking my illustrations from the canto of Ugolino:

> Ce pécheur détourna sa bouche du féroce repas.

Except for the word "détourner," which is quite different from "soulever," the translation gives here the exact meaning, but nothing more: it turns poetry into prose, and familiar prose; it gives us Dante in bedroom slippers. A sight so horrible is ex-

---

preme Ruler still shines on us]. (Author's note) The passage is from the canto of Farinata, *Hell,* x, 102.

73. The description here given strongly suggests the boldly literal method followed by Lamennais' master, fellow Breton, and lifelong friend, Chateaubriand, in his translation of *Paradise Lost,* published in 1836.

pressed in the conversational tone that might be used to invite someone to a stroll or to dinner. Very different is Lamennais:

> De l'horrible pâture ce pécheur souleva sa bouche.

How appropriate is "pâture," which brings before us the nature of the repast, that beastly act, as the poet himself had called it earlier. And in the arrangement of the words and the harmony rising out of them can you not feel something unusual? Lamennais' imagination is struck with horror. It is not only Dante's meaning, but his impression, that lives again in this version. Let us continue the comparison:

Brizeux	*Lamennais*
Puis il commença en ces termes.	Puis il commença.
Mais tu me sembles vraiment florentin, quand je t'entends parler.	Mais, à t'entendre, bien me parais-tu florentin.
Tu dois savoir.	Sache.
De quoi as-tu coutume de pleurer?	De quoi pleureras-tu?
Je me sentais devenir de pierre.	Je fus pétrifié.
Je vis sur quatre visages l'aspect que je devais avoir.	Sur quatre visages je vis mon propre aspect.
Quand il eut ainsi parlé.	Cela dit.
Il reprit le misérable crâne, où ses dents, comme celles d'un chien furieux, entrèrent jusqu'à l'os.	Et renfonça les dents dans le crâne misérable, qu'il broya, comme le chien broie les os.
Tu es bien cruel.	Bien cruel es tu.
Gaddo se jeta et s'étendit à mes pieds.	Gaddo tomba étendu a mes pieds.

[*Hell*, xxxiii, 4–78 *passim*]

It is the translation of a pupil corrected by his master. Frenchmen, in expressing the same thing, tend to agree in the use of the same words and phrases—which seldom happens to Italians, for reasons not to be mentioned here. These two translations are so similar in vocabulary and idioms that the second seems like the first version revised and emended. In appearance the changes are only trifling, but the whole secret of style is in them: proper words substituted for trite phrases like "devenir de pierre"; brief and direct speech instead of useless periphrases such as "tu dois savoir," "De quoi as-tu coutume de pleurer," "l'aspect que je devais avoir," "quand il eut ainsi parlé," etc.; word order dictated by imagination or emotion as "bien cruel es tu," "le crâne misérable," etc.; exquisite art in the expression of accessory ideas, as "la douleur désespérée, qui, seulement d'y penser, m'oppresse le coeur avant que je parle" (Brizeux says, "M'oppresse le coeur en y pensant et avant que je parle"); as "à t'entendre, bien me parais-tu florentin" (Brizeux says, "Tu me sembles vraiment florentin, quand je t'entends parler"); a poetical harmony that strikes your ear with a reminiscence of Dante's harsh energy, as "qu'il broya, comme le chien broie les os,"

che furo all'osso, come d'un can, forti.

that were strong as a dog's upon the bone.—*Hell*, xxxiii, 78.

Add to these merits a certain wholesomeness and chastity of form, far from any suggestion of excessive polish and from bombast. The translator's eye has sought out every delicate beauty, every gradation of feeling. Ugolino, seeing in a dream his own fate and that of his children vaguely foreshadowed in the wolf and its whelps, applies to those animals the human terms "the father and the children" [*Hell*, xxxiii, 35]. "Fatigués me paraissaient le père et les fils," translates Lamennais, and superbly; while Brizeux says prosaically, "Le loup et ses petits me parurent fatigués." Brizeux remained insensible to the heartrending grief in the words "father" and "children," words with double connotations that show at once what Ugolino sees and what his vision reveals to him. A little farther on we read, "Pour nous regarder ainsi, mon père, qu'as tu?" where Dante says:

Tu guardi sì, padre, che hai?

Thou lookest so, father, what ails thee?—*Hell,* xxxiii, 51.

For this touching language, where everything is spontaneous feeling, and there is no thought of logical sequence, Brizeux has substituted a discursive form, a sort of *post hoc, ergo propter hoc,* while Lamennais is stupendously effective: "Père, comme tu regardes! Qu'as-tu?"

The version is preceded by an introduction to the *Divine Comedy,* divided into eight chapters of which the last three are an exposition of the poem's general meaning and an analysis of the individual parts. And the other five chapters? We have been hearing for a long time that "literature is the expression of the individual and of society"; [74] consequently every critic feels today that in speaking of a literary work he must give us the history of the author and his age. Lamennais has chosen this same course: in the first chapter he accordingly gives us a sketch of world history from the fall of the Roman Empire to our own day, in the next two he discusses Dante and his works, and in the last two he expounds the Poet's philosophical and political ideas. In short, these five chapters are designed to answer the question, "What is the content, or subject matter, of the Dantean world?"

In earlier criticism this part was either omitted, or it was offered as a curiosity, as a collection of facts and information. The older criticism considered only the external craftsmanship of writing, qualities often of merely incidental importance which they elevated to the dignity of rules. The subject matter, the content, was either a matter of indifference or was touched

74. The phrase "la littérature est l'expression de la société" was first given general circulation in the first work of the leading theorist of the Catholic reaction in France, *Théorie du pouvoir* (1796) by Louis de Bonald; it was then popularized by Madame de Staël in *De la littérature* (1800) and *De l'Allemagne* (1810). Cf. what De Sanctis says of the French penchant for historical criticism in the essay on Pier delle Vigne.

upon for a show of erudition. Take the famous judgments on *Jerusalem Delivered,* including the judgment of Tasso himself. They are concerned only with unity of action, simplicity of invention, decorum, mores, sentiments, and above all the language and that sort of elocution that passed then for style. A modern, on the other hand, if called upon to judge Tasso, will give you the story of the Crusades, will discourse on the circumstances that led to their being undertaken, on the nature of these circumstances, and so forth; if he is to judge Dante, he will tell you of his life, of Guelfs and Ghibellines, of Popes and Emperors, of Aristotle and St. Thomas. The subject matter, which was secondary with the old criticism, is of primary importance with the new.

Early criticism was rhetorical; modern criticism is a history of facts and doctrines. Now, both rhetoric and history, that is to say general laws and social factors, are preliminary data which may serve as the basis for a critical study, but they are not yet criticism. Rhetoric gives you pure form, and when separated from the subject it degenerates into abstract rules, often arbitrary and accidental, always extrinsic; history gives you pure fact, the abstract content of poetry, the raw and inorganic material which is common to all living at the same time. The ideas and passions which, for instance, are the basis of the *Divine Comedy* can be found also in Brunetto Latini, in Cavalcanti, and in many legends of that time. Why are they immortal in Dante alone? Because Dante alone succeeded in assimilating and transforming that material, shaping a confused and mechanical aggregate into a living organic whole. Therefore the fundamental question for the critic is this: given such times, such ideas, and such passions, in what manner was that material worked out by the poet, in what way did he transform that reality into poetry?

Lamennais does not so much as suspect the existence of this problem. His five chapters are antecedents, the mere data of a problem left unsolved. The abstract content of the poem is reduced to prose, the Dantean world dismembered.

Criticism is the consciousness or the eye of poetry; it is the spontaneous work of genius reproduced as the reflected work of taste. It should not dissolve the poetic universe, but show me the selfsame unity changed into its own rationale, become self-conscious. When Manzoni, for example, first places Don Abbondio or Federico Borromeo [75] on the stage and then, breaking off the narration, pauses to describe his character and the influence his time exerted upon him, he is actually continuing as a critic the work he had begun as a poet. That second part is the same Abbondio or Federico, first created by genius, then recreated by reflection, that is to say by the poet who, having allayed the impulse of his imagination, pauses for a reflective consideration of what he has created. The novel is distinguished from pure poetry by this reflective element which Manzoni introduces almost always in just measure, while in Balzac it goes beyond all limits and often engulfs the poetry. Criticism is thus neither absolute thought nor absolute art, but partakes of both; it is the poetic conception itself viewed from a different vantage point. God created the universe; the philosopher is the critic of God, because true philosophy is the creation re-thought or reflected. Similarly true criticism is the poetic creation as it looks back or is reflected upon itself.

But in order to achieve this, the critic must grasp the question in its essence, must view the poetic material in its successive formative phases—now symbol, now person, here character or passion, there idea or sentiment or image. Lamennais, instead, proceeds like those historians who think they are giving you a philosophical concept of history by writing chapters on religion, institutions, art, science, etc., without realizing that these elements must take their place in the total story, must appear within the facts themselves in their reciprocal interaction, being now cause and now effect. When you abstract them from action you withdraw them from life and history and reduce them to bare concepts. Thus Lamennais, setting out to explain the Dantean

75. Characters in Manzoni's *I Promessi Sposi.*

poetry, instead of reproducing as criticism that image which the poet has externalized as art, begins by annulling it, by dissolving with one puff that magnificent creation into scattered elements—religion, politics, moral philosophy, historical events, etc. He did not take up his pen just after reading and while still moved by the reading. Since it is impossible to mention Dante's name without recalling a multitude of commentators and comments, each of which has dissolved the *Divine Comedy* into pieces and fragments, our distinguished author could not resist the same impulse, having in mind rather the interpreters than the poem itself; and he, too, has decided to take part in that sort of chemical decomposition of the Dantean universe. Thus, instead of an animated and dramatic exposition, he wrote a descriptive dissertation.

Still, this sort of work has its uses. It is of direct help for the intelligence of the poem; and it is of indirect help to criticism by gathering and ascertaining the facts upon which it must be based. Having once set foot in this maze, did Lamennais shed upon it the light of his intelligence? Did he see all the important questions, define them, resolve them? In short, did he attempt to do a serious work?

Here is what, in my opinion, a serious work must do: it must grasp the content of the *Divine Comedy* in its entirety, and analyze it with precision into its constituent elements; it must reject the secondary, frivolous, or pedantic questions on which so many volumes have been written; it must determine the essential questions and arrange them in an order that corresponds to the successive moments of the Dantean world; it must expound lucidly such questions as are now to be considered as results achieved beyond dispute, while clarifying and defining the other questions.

This serious work has not yet been done; and now, after reading Lamennais, I must regretfully repeat, "It has not yet been done." When Schelling said that the study of the Dantean universe could be made into a science, he had in mind a work of this type; this science is still a *desideratum*. For an analytic work of this kind, the Dantean synthesis should already pre-exist in the author's mind; unfortunately, Lamennais set to work without any kind of clear conception of the Dantean unity. Therefore he gropes about, he deals needlessly with points already well treated by others and resolves with a mere yes or no other questions of the greatest importance; and when, as at times, he seems on the point of saying something new and we turn to gaze eagerly at that patch of clear sky, it turns cloudy before our eyes.

When I see a problem discussed by a writer, I ask myself: "In what state was this problem before, and what has become of it now?" Well, Dante problems remain the same; Lamennais has written on them without leaving a trace. Why write a life of Dante? He could have referred the reader to Cesare Balbo, or even to Villemain, who considered him from only one side, but well. The biography of Dante, as the story of the events in his personal life, is an aspect of the subject that has already been exhausted. There are still a few factual questions to settle, as for instance the time when Dante began the *Divine Comedy*, but Lamennais did not bother with them; he merely gathered facts of common knowledge. The real life of Dante still to be written is the story of his soul, the definition of his mind, his character, his passions; it is his full-face portrait instead of the profile which writers have sketched up until now. This is the new aspect of the subject: Lamennais did not see it.

Of what use is an analytical bibliography of his works? A discussion of the *Convivio* should give us an exposition of Dante's poetics; a discussion of his lyrics should show us the first form in which his poetic mind was revealed, and so on. These are the points to be investigated; all the rest is trite. Did we need Lamennais to learn that singing is natural to man and that poetry is therefore the chanted word, a point he amplifies with a bit of rhetoric, as if this were not one of those points that must be referred to as conclusions, without expatiating upon them? He speaks of the mysticism of Dantean love, which is scarcely worth the trouble after Opitz [Kopisch] and Ozanam. That word "mysticism" has been abused; what matters more is to show underneath that mysticism the profoundly real passion which gives it movement and life. He encounters a problem of capital importance, Rossetti's system of Dantean political symbolism. He accepts it, affirming rather than proving it, overlooking the serious objections raised by Schlegel, and repeating some of the trivial remarks made by Rossetti and Aroux. And yet this was no place for a simple affirmation or rejection. It would have been worthy of Lamennais' talents to go resolutely into that question and settle it definitely, sifting the truth from all the exaggerations to which the Italian commentator and the Frenchman were driven by their systemizing, and which led them to make of the *Divine Comedy* a political charade.

In the first, fourth, and fifth chapters we catch glimpses of new horizons; the style is more colorful and lively. Yet the author's obvious preconceptions often suggest that he has in mind rather our own times than those of Dante. Are the Catholic and Germanic elements the only factors in modern civilization, or is there also a Latin element? Can Catholicism be reconciled with liberty? Was the Papacy favorable to Italian freedom? These questions are of paramount importance, no doubt; but the *Divine Comedy* is here no longer the real theme, but a pretext for Lamennais to put in his last word, before dying, on the passionate debates that so agitate us at the present moment. And since these are incidental questions, it is not surprising that Lamennais does not treat them in the definitive sort of manner that would preclude rebuttal; his remarks are outbursts of an indignant soul against the wretched present, rather than a discussion offered with a serious purpose. In short, it would appear that Lamennais was prevented by his death from establishing more clearly the design of his work, from organizing the parts more accurately, and from giving to the questions discussed that thorough development, that final touch of perfection which could make us declare, "Here are truths solidly established!"

But although his work lacks that lofty perspective which gives us an insight into the subject and a grasp of all its living parts, it is never wanting in the superficial qualities of style, clearness, efficacy, and brilliance. For instance, the scientific doctrine on which Dante's *Paradise* is constructed is expounded with great lucidity, a quality lacking in Göschel, though Göschel's work on the same subject is very profound and clearly worked out. That essential trait of the *Divine Comedy,* of summing up the past and foreshadowing the future, is set forth with a vivacity and freshness of expression that seems incredible when one reflects on the age of the writer. "The poem is at once a tomb and a cradle: the magnificent tomb of a world that is dying, the cradle of a world about to bloom; a portico between two temples, the temple of the past and the temple of the future." The observation is not new, as it has been made, to mention only Frenchmen, by Labitte; [76] but Lamennais discovers that trait in his own way and describes it with the freshness of a first impression, giving it a splendid form that fixes it in our mind.

In these five chapters, then, the author tells us who the Poet was and what the material was upon which he worked. But we must not forget that all this, to which modern criticism attaches so much importance, is only raw material, scattered members awaiting the breath of life to shape themselves into an organic whole, into a man. We have not yet entered the temple of art; as yet we have no criticism. In what way did Dante work this material and fashion from it a world? That is the crux of the question.

If Lamennais had perceived that, it would have formed the material of his five chapters. In Dante's time philosophical and political doctrines had penetrated every aspect of social life and given rise to what is called the Catholic world. This was the

76. A similar image had been employed by Mazzini in an article on Lamennais, in which the French writer was compared to "a giant [rising] between a world in decay and a world in infancy . . . bounding over the abyss that separates the tomb from the cradle." (Giuseppe Mazzini, "Lamennais" (1839) in *Scritti editi e inediti,* Edizione Nazionale, Imola, Galeati, xvii, 352.)

common basis of reality to poet as to philosopher, and out of it grew a distinctive philosophy which Ritter properly calls Christian philosophy, and a poetry different from that of the ancients. If Lamennais had perceived this he would not have given us a mere abstract exposition of the doctrines of the time, but would have shown us a world sprung to life as the incarnation of those ideas; he would have outlined the essential characteristics of that world, its esthetic qualities, its still vague and embryonic ideal of which we see scattered and fleeting traces in the "Legends" and which is destined to come to full development when submitted to the scrutiny of a man capable of understanding and feeling it. Behold that man: the world becomes art, becomes the *Divine Comedy*. At this point the author, touching lightly upon Dante's life, would show us the qualities of his poetic intelligence, his character, and the influence which his misfortunes and his passions exerted upon him. Having thus determined the essential qualities of the subject and of the man treating it, he would give us the real *datum* of the problem: given "such a subject" and "such an artist," in what way was the material elaborated?

Since the author had expounded the antecedents of the problem, I was able to show how such an enquiry should have been conducted. As for the problem itself, there is no trace of it; the author has no inkling of it and blinks it utterly. I shall therefore make no attempt to state how, in my opinion, the problem should have been solved, for I do not presume to substitute myself for the author; I will only point out that since the author failed to rise to this elevated viewpoint, his last three chapters could only be just what they are, a summary of the three canticles. The content previously expounded as bare fact and which should now reappear as artifact, is forgotten; he continues as if these preceding five chapters did not exist. He starts over on an empty sort of general discussion, throwing in some observations on the immortality of the soul, on the eternity of punishment, on predestination, etc., which have no connection with the rest and no application to the subject. Then comes the summary, that is to say an analytical exposition of the three canticles. What does he make of this? With only a vague and confused conception of the poem as a whole and of the separate canticles, the critic follows the Poet step by step: he passes over some things that seem to him indifferent or unimportant, and lingers over certain others that seem to him beautiful. It is a critique in the style of Ginguené, of Sismondi, of Bouterwek, a criticism of details. It is like a journey on which you follow every turn of the road without purpose or plan: you notice one thing, admire another, but never rise high enough to understand "del cammin la mente" [the journey's mind—*Purgatory*, III, 56], as Dante puts it in his bold metaphor.[77]

This kind of piecemeal criticism was the *non plus ultra* of the old school, and Laharpe gave a splendid example of it in France. But how far superior is Lamennais in this field! In the old school impressions seldom remained spontaneous and natural; they were perverted by rhetoric, by preconceived rules, by a conventional and affected taste, and by a certain pedantic subtlety that was not content with the simple chaste beauty that comes quite naturally to our attention, but delighted in subtle interpretations and by excessive embellishment of the text adulterated and inflated it. Lamennais is free from any preconceptions and relies on his refined feeling and exquisite taste. This is how he proceeds. After sketching the setting in a few quick strokes he follows the Poet, relating and summarizing the action. In his rapid summaries—where perforce you find many gaps—whenever he meets with something that appeals to him he pauses, as if enticed by its charm, and quotes the entire passage. Then while still warm from his response to the impression he comes out with exclamations of admiration, casting here and there a wealth of extremely delicate observations which constitute the truly original part of

77. De Sanctis is using words cited from Dante to convey his own thought. In its context the line quoted is always taken to mean "searching" or "questioning his mind about the road," a perfectly literal meaning and not a bold metaphor.

the book. Observe, among other things, his notes on Farinata and Guido da Montefeltro. He had a keen understanding of the Poet's swift concise style, his manner of painting in bold strokes, the great number of secondary ideas he contrives to awaken in your mind, the variety of his emotions and characters, his skill at preparing a situation and developing it. No one knows better than he how to appreciate Dante's union of great power with great simplicity, his clear delineations in which there remains so much that is vague and fluctuating.

Some of his observations, and these are the most precious, while directed toward this or that passage have a more general significance. Thus, speaking of Farinata, he tells us how the Poet portrays his characters: "Not a single reflection; a few bold strokes of his brush, a short dialogue, every word of which bares the soul to its depth, and the picture is complete." In connection with Ser Brunetto, the author shows us the "human" side of the *Divine Comedy:* "Within the damned soul one can still discern the human being. How could anyone bear otherwise the frightful account of all these torments? It would only rouse a feeling of disgust and horror, and the book would fall from our hands." Oderisi says:

> La vostra nominanza è color d'erba
>   Che viene e va . . . .
> Your reputation is as the color of grass, which comes and
>   goes . . . .—*Purgatory,* XI, 115.

The author uses this text to show us one of the most striking traits of the penitent souls, their calm in the midst of suffering, their state of being "contente nel fuoco" [contented in the fire— *Hell,* I, 118], as Dante calls them. "Oderisi does not say 'our reputation' but 'your reputation.' In the world where he is purifying himself before rising to God, the world he has left behind no longer touches him; it appears to him as it would appear to a dweller from another sphere, freed of passion or illusion, with serene compassion; and this serenity amid sufferings which they desire and love as the necessary condition for the infinite good which shall follow, constitutes the principal characteristic of the state of souls in this intermediate region. A single word sufficed to mark the cleavage between two ways of life so closely linked and yet so dissimilar."

Since Oderisi's calm is a quality shared by all the penitent souls, Lamennais glimpsed here the very thing lacking in his work, which death perhaps prevented him from supplying, namely, a general conception of Purgatory and a general account of the penitent souls. He gives only a sketch, but a very beautiful one. "The tone of this canticle is in fundamental contrast with that of the preceding one. It possesses a certain quality that is sweet and sad like twilight, airy like a dream. The violent impulses of the soul have found appeasement. The material sufferings here resemble those of Hell and yet the impression is altogether different. They arouse tender pity rather than terror and bitter anguish. The penitent souls not only accept their suffering because they recognize its justice, but they desire it because they know that through it they shall be healed and that in its transitory pain they have a presentiment of a joy everlasting. Hence their attitude which is somehow calm, tranquil, melancholy, and serene. Take away from life on earth all uncertainty, doubt, and fear, but leave in it, together with its miseries, hope to console them and a full faith that one can attain the goal that hope points out, and you will have Purgatory as Dante paints it. And this is so because in the last analysis Purgatory, Hell, Heaven, to the extent that we can really conceive or feel them, are simply the diverse states of men on earth, are the world we live in, with its mixture of virtues and vices, joys and sorrows, light and darkness, of which the other world is indeed only a projection in a loftier and grander sphere." Obviously Lamennais lacked neither an understanding of his task nor the powers of synthesis necessary to execute it, as the above passage shows. But these are only flashes; these extremely penetrating comments, touching on some of the more essential parts of the *Purgatory,*

remain at loose ends, without premises and without consequences, and hence they remain sterile.

No less valuable are his observations of detail; while some are
vague or commonplace others can be called discoveries. He is the
first to perceive why the Cavalcanti episode was inserted into
Farinata's story. "The more touching this scene becomes, the
more vividly it brings out the character of Farinata. For him the
scene simply did not take place: completely absorbed in the bitter
feeling aroused in his proud soul by the words of Dante, he saw
nothing, heard nothing." Equally keen is Lamennais' observation
that Farinata's patriotism tempered the asperity of his character,
that his was a pride without harshness: "Without weakening
Farinata's character, the poet tempers its asperity by showing in
the partisan, in the factional leader, something even stronger than
hate—the sweet, the holy love for his country."

Here is another very delicate observation. Everybody remembers the admirable simile,

> Come le pecorelle escon dal chiuso . . . .
> As the sheep come forth from the fold . . . .—*Purgatory,* III,
> 79.

"Notice," says Lamennais, "what a calm and peaceful morning
light these pastoral images shed upon regions which yet are
consecrated to tears, and how the innocence of these simple,
sweet, and placid creatures is reflected upon the souls still sick,
still suffering, but assured now of possessing, in the bosom of an
eternal peace, a happiness unalterable. It is in these hidden con-
formities which one feels but cannot express, so delicate and
fleeting are their shadings, that lies the inexhaustible charm of a
work of real genius." Lamennais is right; the poet does not seek
out these secret relationships, they simply flow from his pen. And
the great critic, who also has his share of spontaneity, does not go
looking for them, but feels them in the very act of reading.

To be sure, not everything is of that level of perfection. At
times you meet with vague impressions which the author did not

have the patience to reduce to clear and precise terms. Here is what he says about the famous phrase "guarda e passa" [do thou look and pass on—*Hell,* III, 49]: "What indignation, what wrath, could weigh upon these souls as heavily as this scorn?" He concludes his analysis of Farinata as follows: "If these are not beauties equal to any that poetry ever offered, what are they then?" Often he says, "You can see that the Poet felt indignation, scorn, wrath, or bitterness, etc."

All this is a worthless criticism made of catch-phrases. At times he delights in drawing parallels, and I loathe criticism by this kind of analogy which critics down to the present day have so often abused, because it either confines itself to generalities or it leads to absurd consequences. When, for instance, Lamennais, and Chateaubriand [78] before him, compare Dante's Lucifer to Milton's Satan, and prefer the latter to the former, they fail to observe that in this instance the parallel does not apply, because the characters are based on two essentially different conceptions. Lamennais, with all his partiality for Dante, states that Dante's real Lucifer is Capaneus. But if Dante could express so successfully in Capaneus the sort of sublimity we admire in Milton's Satan, why did he not portray his Lucifer with equal sublimity? This should have led Lamennais to suspect that Dante had his own good reasons for doing as he did. What parallel can be established between the description of light by Milton and the one by Dante? [79] There is an essential difference of situation, of impression, and therefore of style.

At times the author's impression is so vivid that it goes beyond the poetry, continues it in its own way, and adds feelings and images extraneous to it: he forgets Dante and expresses himself. Poetry is the soul's oblivion before the object of its contemplation; criticism is the soul's oblivion before poetry. Lamennais goes beyond these limits, yields to his emotions, and relieves his spirit overburdened with bitterness. Dante says,

78. In *Génie du Christianisme,* IIe partie, livre III, ch. 9.
79. *Paradise Lost,* III, 1; *Purgatory,* I, 13.

Libertà va cercando ch'è si cara . . . .

He goes on seeking liberty which is so dear . . . .—*Purga-tory*, I, 71.

The critic is deeply moved by a word which to him, already close to the grave, epitomizes all his life, his dreams of liberty, his hopes, his brief joys, his cruel disappointments, his invincible faith in the future. "Alas!" he cries out—as a man, not as a critic—"what are we, in every sense, if not poor wretches who go on seeking liberty: liberty of the mind enslaved by prejudice and ignorance, liberty of the heart enslaved by passions, liberty of the body delivered to the whims of insolent masters; liberty in all spheres, intellectual, moral, political? What are our human societies, what is the world, if not a black tomb in which tyranny under a thousand hideous aspects chains us to dead bones?"

I have not the heart to call this a failing. This is not the stupid subjectivism of shallow minds, incapable of immersing and absorbing themselves in the task before them; it is the failing of a beautiful soul, a melancholy introversion, an occasional turning of the eyes away from the Middle Ages toward the present. There are certain passages of this kind which grip your heart. Pope Adrian, speaking of Alagia, says in closing,

E questa sola m'è di là rimasa.

And she alone remains to me yonder.—*Purgatory*, XIX, 145.

Lamennais adds, "What sadness in this brief, simple phrase which ends the Pope's story, as life ends, with solitude and emptiness!" "And what a melancholy comment," I add in my turn, "and what simplicity amid such sadness!"

Lamennais wrote these words a few days before his death. It is regrettable that death should have kept him from completing such a weighty task and bringing it to perfection. Even without considering the lacunae and the parts left unfinished, his style sometimes gives me the impression, especially in the early chapters, of a summary rather than of an exposition; it is a form roughly sketched and tentative, which he surely expected to polish. Old but still vigorous, he was struck down by death at his battle station, fighting on his last day with the faith and vigor of youth. Few can say as could Lamennais, "My whole life has been a battle, an arduous and painful battle for the good of humanity." May many of you enjoy a youth comparable to the sublime old age of Dante's translator!

Biographical Glossary

Alfieri, Vittorio (1749–1803), the greatest Italian tragedian.

Aroux, Eugene (1783–1859), French translator of Dante, who drew heavily on Rossetti in studies presenting Dante as an Albigensian heretic, and even as pastor of an Albigensian church in Florence!

Balbo, Count Cesare (1789–1853), Italian historian and statesman, who wrote a *Vita di Dante* (Torino, 1839).

Béranger, Pierre Jean de (1780–1857), French song writer whose verses enjoyed an extraordinary vogue during the first half of the nineteenth century.

Berchet, Giovanni (1783–1851), Italian patriot and poet, author of *romanze,* in the style of German ballads, lyric-narrative poems inspired by hatred for the domestic and foreign tyrants of his country.

Biagioli, Niccolò Giosafatte (1768–1830), Italian man of letters. He spent most of his adult life in Paris, where he published his commentary on the *Divine Comedy* (1818–19), later frequently reprinted in Italy.

Bouterwek, Friedrich (1766–1828), German philosopher and critic, professor of philosophy at Göttingen, where he published numerous philosophical studies, novels, poems, and a twelve-volume *Geschichte der neuer Poesie und Beredsamkeit* (1801–19).

Brizeux, Auguste (1803–1858), French poet whose translation of the

151

Divine Comedy (1842) was rather well received by French critics.

Cavalca, Domenico (1270–1342), saintly Dominican monk and prolific writer of edifying works, notably the *Vite dei Santi Padri* (Lives of the Holy Fathers).

Cavalcanti, Guido (1255–1300), the leading Florentine poet before Dante and Dante's closest friend.

Cesari, Antonio (1760–1828), devout priest, tireless scholar and lexicographer, author of numerous religious writings, as well as critical and erudite works. His series of dialogues *Sulle Bellezze della Divina Commedia* (1824–26) contributed greatly to reawaken the interest of Italians in Dantean studies.

Cino da Pistoia (1270–1336), famous jurist, teacher of Petrarch at Bologna, and highly praised as a poet by Dante.

Colombo, Michele (1747–1836), priest, tutor in several noble families. His *Lezioni sulle doti d'una colta favella* (1812) won a prize from the Accademia della Crusca and was frequently reprinted.

Costa, Paolo (1771–1836), Italian man of letters, author of plays, poems, and translations. He prepared in collaboration with Marchetti a commentary on the *Divine Comedy.*

Dall'Ongaro, Francesco (1808–1873), Italian patriot, poet, and playwright, who gave a series of lectures on the *Divine Comedy* in Trieste in 1846 and again in Brussels in 1855.

D'Aquino, Carlo (1654–1740), Neapolitan Jesuit who published a Latin version of the *Divine Comedy, La Commedia di D.A. trasportata in verso latino eroico da C. d'A. della Compagnia di Gesu, con l'aggiunta del testo italiano e di brevi annotazioni* (Napoli, Mosca, 1728).

Enzo (1225?–1272), son of Frederick II; early Italian poet.

Fazio degli Uberti (fl. c. 1350), grandson of Farinata; scholar and poet whose works include an encyclopedic poem, *Dittamondo,* patterned after the *Divine Comedy.*

Foscolo, Ugo (1778–1827), the great Italian poet, during his exile in London wrote a number of studies on Dante, most important of which was the *Discorso sul testo della Commedia di Dante* (London, 1825), and also a commentary on the *Divine Comedy,* published posthumously by Mazzini (London, 1842).

Frederick II (1194–1250), Holy Roman Emperor and King of Sicily; Italian poet.

Ginguené, Pierre L. (1748–1816), French critic, author of the first nine volumes of a fourteen-volume *Histoire Littéraire d'Italie* later completed by Francesco Salfi (Paris, 1811–19).

Gioberti, Vincenzo (1801–1852), Italian philosopher and statesman. His pages of literary criticism, scattered in his philosophical and political writings, place him in the front rank of Italian literary critics of the first half of the nineteenth century.

Goeschel, Karl F. (1784–1862), disciple of Hegel, author of numerous works on Dante stressing the mystical interpretation of the *Divine Comedy*. In 1853 he delivered a course of lectures on Dante before the Evangelical Association of Berlin, in the presence of the King of Prussia.

Guinicelli, Guido (between 1230 and 1240–1274), native of Bologna but founder of the "Tuscan" school of poetry.

Kannegiesser, K. L. (1781–1861), German translator of and commentator on the *Divine Comedy,* whose translation, first published in 1809–21, was frequently reprinted.

Kléber, Jean Baptiste (1753–1800), one of the greatest French generals of the Revolutionary and Napoleonic periods. He was so imposing in stature that he was called by his comrades "God Mars in uniform."

Kopisch, August (1799–1853), German painter and poet, author of a German translation of the *Divine Comedy* in blank verse (Berlin, 1842).

Labitte, Charles (1816–1845), French teacher and writer, frequent contributor to the *Revue des Deux Mondes,* which in September, 1842, published his study "La *Divine Comédie* avant Dante: les prédécesseurs et les inspirateurs de Dante."

La Harpe, Jean François de (1739–1803), French critic and playwright, whose lectures at the Lycée in Paris were published, in part posthumously, under the title *Cours de littérature ancienne et moderne* (1799–1805), and were often reprinted later.

Lamartine, Alphonse (1790–1869), French poet, historian, and statesman, discussed Dante in "Notes sur le Dante," published in *Le Siècle* (10 Dec. 1856) and later republished, first in *Cours familier de Littérature* and then in *Trois poètes italiens: Dante, Pétrarque, le Tasse.*

Lamennais, Félicité R. de (1782–1854), French priest and reformer, copious writer on philosophical and political subjects, devoted the last few years of his life to a study and translation of the *Divine Comedy,* published posthumously in 1855, and sympathetically reviewed in the last essay of the present volume.

Landino, Cristoforo (1424–1504), Florentine humanist, lecturer on Dante at the University of Florence, and author of the commentary in the first Florentine edition of the *Divine Comedy* (Firenze, 1481).

Lapo degli Uberti, son of Farinata and Imperial Vicar at Verona.

Latini, Brunetto (c. 1220–1294), Florentine scholar, poet, statesman, and teacher of Dante.

Lombardi, Baldassare (18th century), Franciscan monk, author of an edition of the *Divine Comedy, La Divina Commedia nuovamente corretta, spiegata e difesa* (Rome, 1791), often reprinted in the nineteenth century and praised by Foscolo and Witte.

Magalotti, Lorenzo (1637–1712), brilliant, versatile Florentine poet, critic, scientist, and diplomat, many of whose works were published posthumously, including his *Commenti sui primi canti dell'Inferno* (Milan, 1819).

Maiano, Dante da (second half of 13th century), a mediocre Florentine imitator of the "Sicilian" school, who wrote also in Provençal.

Manfred (1232?–1266), King of Sicily, son of Frederick II, Italian poet.

Marchetti, Giovanni (1790–1852), collaborated with Paolo Costa on a commentary on the *Divine Comedy,* and prepared the introductory essay, "Discorso su la prima e principale allegoria di Dante" (Bologna, 1819).

Metastasio. See Trapassi, Pietro.

Nettement, Alfred F. (1805–1869), French critic of militantly Catholic and Legitimist orientation, author of numerous works of literary history, including *Histoire de la littérature française sous la Restauration* (Paris, 1852) and *Histoire de la littérature française sous la royauté de juillet* (Paris, 1854).

Ozanam, Antoine F. (1813–1853), French critic and Christian apologist, born at Milan and one of the founders of the charitable Société de Saint Vincent de Paul. Professor of foreign literatures at the Sorbonne, he was author of numerous works on Italian medieval culture, including the extremely important *Dante et la philosophie catholique au XIII siècle* (Paris, 1839). In 1840 and 1845 he devoted his course to the *Divine Comedy.*

Passavanti, Jacopo (1300–1357), Dominican monk, famous as a preacher and as teacher of philosophy and theology. As a writer he is remembered for his *Specchio di Vera Penitenza* (Mirror of True Penance), a treatise on how to prepare for confession. By its numerous stories related to illustrate the vices and virtues discussed, this work places Passavanti among the best storytellers of the fourteenth century, after Boccaccio.

Pellico, Silvio (1789–1854), Italian playwright and patriot, whose tragedy *Francesca da Rimini,* presented in Milan in 1818, enjoyed great popularity, more for its patriotic overtones than for its artistic merits. Later he became even more famous for his *Le Mie Prigioni,* a story of the fifteen years' imprisonment which he suffered for his patriotism, and which he bore with exemplary patience and Christian resignation.

Quinet, Edgar (1803–1875), French critic, poet, and historian, professor of Southern literatures at the Collège de France, where he delivered lectures on the great Italian poets, later published under the title *Les Révolutions d'Italie* (Paris, 1848–52).

Rienzo, Cola di—not *da* (1313–1354), the eloquent but politically inept leader of the short-lived Roman Republic re-established in 1347 while the Papal See was at Avignon.

Ritter, Heinrich (1791–1869), German philosopher, professor of philosophy at the universities of Berlin, Kiel, and Göttingen, author of numerous works, including a voluminous *Geschichte der Philosophie* (1829–53), which was translated into all European languages.

Rossetti, Gabriele (1783–1854), Italian patriot and poet, father of Dante Gabriel, William Michael, and Christina, during his exile in England wrote studies on the *Divine Comedy,* exaggerating the antipapal spirit of Dante, which were widely discussed at the time: *Dello Spirito antipapale,* etc. (London, 1832); *Il mistero dell'amor platonico nel medio evo, derivato dai misteri antichi* (London, 1840); *La Beatrice di Dante* (London, 1842).

Saint-Marc Girardin, François A. (1801–1873), French statesman and scholar, professor first of history, then of poetry at the Sorbonne, and Member of the Academy.

Schelling, Friedrich Wilhelm Joseph von (1775–1854), discussed Dante in his essay "Ueber Dante in philosophischer Beziehung," in *Kritisches Journal der Philosophie,* Vol. II, No. 3 (1802), pp. 35–50.

Schlegel, August Wilhelm von (1767–1845), German poet, translator, and critic, brother of the more famous Karl Wilhelm Friedrich, refuted Rossetti's thesis in "Dante, Pétrarque et Boccace, à propos de l'ouvrage de M. Rossetti," in *Revue des Deux Mondes,* VII (1836), 400–418.

Schlegel, Karl Wilhelm Friedrich von (1772–1829), standard-bearer, with his older brother August Wilhelm, of Romantic criticism, discussed Dante in *Geschichte der alten und neuen Literatur* (1815).

Sismondi, Jean Charles Léonard de (1773–1842), famous Swiss historian who gave a series of lectures on Southern European literatures, and later published them under the title *Littérature du Midi de l'Europe* (1813, 4 vols.).

Trapassi, Pietro (1698–1782), Italian dramatist, court poet at Vienna, and probably the greatest of all authors of operatic librettos, if one is to judge by their number and variety, the quality of the music they inspired, and their intrinsic value as verse.

Troya, Carlo (1784–1858), Italian medievalist, author of *Del Veltro allegorico di Dante* (London, 1825).

Vellutello, Alessandro (early 16th century–1566?), Tuscan scholar who prepared commentaries on Petrarch's *Canzoniere* (1525) and on the *Divine Comedy* (1544).

Villemain, Abel François (1790–1870), French scholar and statesman, professor of French eloquence at the Sorbonne. He discussed Dante in the first volume of his *Cours de littérature française* (1828), pp. 296–317, and in his *Tableau de la littérature au Moyen Age* (1846).

Wegele, F. X. (1823–1897), German historian, professor at the universities of Jena and Wurzburg; his first important work, *Dante Alighieri's Leben und Werke kulturgeschichtlich dargestellt* was published at Jena in 1852.

Witte, K. (1800–1883), one of the greatest of German Dante scholars.

Index

Names in italics are of characters in the *Divine Comedy*.

De Sanctis on Dante

Francesco De Sanctis, the founder of modern Italian literary criticism, is more and more widely coming to be considered one of the finest critical intelligences of modern times. English readers, who have so far been acquainted with him only through the *History of Italian Literature,* will welcome this translation of his critical essays on Dante. For though the *History* is a masterpiece of its kind, the Dante essays more clearly demonstrate De Sanctis' ability in the task he could do surpassingly well—the interpretation and reconstruction of literary characters. Subsequent critics have enriched our knowledge concerning Dante's times, his ideas, and his culture, but the modern student of Dante must still begin with De Sanctis' masterly interpretations of Francesca, Farinata, and other great figures in the *Divine Comedy*.

De Sanctis' essays are filled with brilliant insights and with admirable critical expositions of individual passages. Few critics have been as sensitive to the way in which Dante creates his magnificent effects with the particular word or phrase which transforms a whole passage or reveals a unique personality.

These essays will be of value not only to those especially interested in Dante but also to estheticians and literary critics in other fields. A. C. Bradley almost alone among English critics is a first-rate representative of Hegelian criticism, which is grounded in historical and

Continued on back flap